For Mike (an author),

   May you enjoy the reading and the chuckles provided by the illustrator...

      Sincerely,

      Lillian M. Juditz

The School

By

Lillian Mickley Juditz

Illustrations by Thomas Corle

Book Design by Thomas Corle

Pine Manor Farm Press

Harrisburg, Pennsylvania

Printed in the United States of America

Our Thanks to...

Vicki Juditz Kirschenbaum, the National Storyteller, who is our daughter. She was the first reader of each chapter, often frowned as she read, and gave us sound advice to improve the writing.

Ruthe F. Craley who was often the patient second reader of each chapter, a teacher for many years in public schools-no error in grammar, no misplaced spelling has ever escaped her eagle eye.

Robert E. Juditz, my late husband, who brought to speech contests the expertise of Toastmasters International.

To Tom Corle, who found the essence of each chapter and expressed it eloquently in a few strokes of his illustrator's brush.

and to

Our Production Coordinator, Georg R. Sheets, who led us through the maze of book creation (and wrote our deadlines in concrete.)

TABLE OF CONTENTS

No one had told me the 90's would not
be nice.

I mean, here we were supposed to be in some won-
derfully new electronic time, and there was tobacco juice all
over the floors.

If this were such an enlightened era, how come students didn't know how to set a table? I gave instructions to
a talented art student to prepare the program cover for A.R.
Gurney's THE DINING ROOM; the cover came back with
the spoon on the left! The knife and fork on the right, and
she had not meant the cover to be satirical.

If this were the age of the greatest medical advance,
why was a Freshman girl spitting in my waste basket, and
another Freshman girl, Harmoney Wells, sitting at my desk,
saying, "Hell, Mrs. J. I'm eight months pregnant–those
damned seats are too small for me. I'M SITTING HERE!"

And if this were the time of "educational reform",
why was the Principal blackmailing me into leaving?

On any ordinary school day there was little time for
philosophical reflection, but when I did have a few spare
moments I found myself thinking: this is uncivilized, this is
the wrong way to do things, this is not making sense; something has happened to the public school that is dangerous.

By January of 1993, 1 had been at Bexley Hills High
School for more than 26 years, had always been given a
satisfactory rating, sometimes even a commendable rating.

True, there were "incidents" in my dossier: the event of two students stealing my keys and flushing them down a toilet; the case of the boy who had taken a stone from the windowsill plant and fired it at a front row bully; the girl who had set fire to a piece of paper on her way back from the pencil sharpener. But overall I had a clean record.

If I had made no close friends, administratively speaking, during those 26-plus years, I had made no enemies, either. Which of course is to say, I was not much of a politician. I was not a Union leader, either. I was a faithful Union MEMBER. I was careful to go through channels on innovative projects. It had required four years' worth of precisely worded applications and interviews to make Speech a course obligatory for graduation. As it so happened, on the fourth try the state mandate for COMMUNICATION AS A NUMBER ONE GOAL IN EVERY HIGH SCHOOL CURRICULUM won the day for me. The Principal of Bexley in that decade had actually thanked me.

But back to the "blackmailing Principal". One morning in mid-January of 1993 I was called to the Principal's office to discuss my evaluation and aspects of the benchmark goals. The latter phrase was a euphemism for "trouble". I was almost sixty-four years old. There was no mandatory retirement age, but 1993 was the first big year of the state "Meadows Bill"; teachers were being given monetary incentives to "fly out the window". Mid-January was the time when principals had to prepare the budget–which meant release enough teachers through attrition to conform to District Budget Policy.

"Mrs. Juditz, it's time we had a little heart to heart talk", Mr. Harvey the Principal was saying.

I made no comment.

"Now I have noted you've been having some problems with the 9th Grade English classes..."

In the budget crunch of the mid-80's I had been asked to add two Track Two English classes to my schedule "as a temp-orary measure". Track Two was a dumping ground for discipline cases, immigrant transfer students, and some hitherto uniden-tified students with learning difficulties.

I thought back to the winter when I had come from professional broadcasting to teach Communication at Bexley, but more importantly to keep in place the co-curric-ular program—almost the only one of its kind in the state—encompassing three grade levels of speech, a disci-pline in theatre arts, along with speech and drama contests, a Drama Club with repertory theatre events, two annual full-length main stage plays that filled an auditorium for 1200 persons, and Children's Theatre for presentation at the District elementary schools.

"I'm afraid, Mrs. Juditz," Mr. Harvey continued, "unless we can work out some special strategies, I really can't give you a Satisfactory Rating..."

Odd, I found myself thinking. Mr. Wheeler, the Assistant Principal who prepared most of the classroom evaluations for Mr. Harvey, had made a point of letting me know he liked my special strategy of a weekly newsletter for each student: details about homework, tests, reading assignments, vocabulary-words-of-the-week. Not only that, Mr. Wheeler had expressed much enthusiasm for my Progress Chart–an outsized piece of colorful construction paper with hundreds of tiny squares for keeping track of student merits awarded for neatly written homework, extra good grades on tests, on-time arrival to class, exemplary behavior in class, etc., etc. About every five weeks or so, students with the highest number of points would win small fun prizes–bright notebooks, funky pens and pencils, erasers, stickers. With the escalating prices of the late 80's, each Awards Day cost me about $25.00.

At this point I was thinking, surely you jest, Mr. Harvey. What you're really blathering about is your budget. Positive input from Mr. Wheeler or no, you, Mr. Harvey want me gone. For my salary you can hire two first-year teachers, and with a little luck, one might be an assistant basketball coach.

Mr. Harvey, with his round, metal-frame spectacles–too small for his large, round, shiny face–had paused to glance down at the evaluation form. Now, with a slight smirk and pursed lips, he was looking at me once more.

By this time I found myself remembering that my daughter, a graduate of Bexley, had said repeatedly during the past year, AFTER her visit to my classes to explain filming of national TV commercials, "You ought to quit, Mom. Those kids are unreachable. They have an attention span of eight seconds. It's EXHAUSTING working with them!"

"Mr. Harvey," I said finally, using direct eye contact and a polite smile, "I really don't need this. I am planning to retire at the end of this season. I'm sending my papers to the District Office."

"Oh!", said Mr. Harvey. The smirk was gone. "I had wondered why you hadn't sent in your intent before, since it's a good year to go."

I recalled there had been a directive sent around to remind all staff it was time to state intent about retiring, transferring, asking for sabbatical leave. Before that January morning I had really given little thought to the advantages of "flying out the window" via the Meadows Bill and leaving Bexley. I suppose I thought I would stay forever. My Uncle Bill, near the middle of a school year when he discovered he had a terminal illness, decided to begin the second semester at his school and taught until April of that year, leaving up-to-the-close-of-school lesson plans for his substitute.

"Well, in that case," Mr. Harvey was continuing, "I will simply put down a Satisfactory Rating, and we'll just forget about these other items."

He snapped shut the file. I could tell he was peeved about being passed over with the intent papers, yet relieved about having dropped one more long-term teacher to meet the budget. I was at the $50,000 level, counting my extra duty fees. This amount would be poor pickings in most other professional worlds; it was substantial for a teacher in the Keystone State. Mr. Harvey, of course was paid $70,000, and the Superintendent (who always read his speech at commencement ceremonies and sometimes got lost in the reading) was paid $98,000. In the mid-80's, as the Bexley school population dwindled, the class sizes grew larger; the administrative staff of South Shore schools tripled. Such have been the "school reforms" of many districts in the '90's.

Why am I writing this book about the school? I once saw a billboard that proclaimed: "School is everybody's business". That's true, but Mr. J.Q. Public doesn't know the first thing about it. I read, hear comments: schools are too expensive, too elaborate; teachers are hard to fire, and they have all summer off; teachers are incompetent–I wouldn't put up with people like that in my business; my kids' clothes are stolen, my kid is picked on; SCHOOL IS NOT SAFE! School does not prepare anyone for much of anything_half the stuff these kids have to learn is useless. WE NEED TO GET BACK TO BASICS!

A majority of the persons with these firm opinions have never been back to school since they left as students. On "Back to School Night" those sections with the largest number of students who have the most discipline problems and the lowest grades have almost no parents present; honor sections, on the other hand, usually have mother, father and grandma for every student. I want the reader to know what school is like, what goes on during an ordinary day.

Bexley Hills High School (not its real name) is a suburban high school. It has a mostly white, mostly middle income school population. It also has a growing number of poor families and a much smaller number of students whose homes are very large mansions. Bexley has all of the problems of other high schools across America, but not to the same degree.

Critics of the American public school system, depending on their age, represent a wide spectrum of school image: beginning with the one-room "little red school house with outdoor privy," circa 1910; through the impressive three-story brownstone Junior High School, named for a general of WW II; on to an inner City school of more recent vintage, where graffiti on the battered front door reads, "f-you all ye who enter here..."

If school is everybody's business, then everybody has a responsibility to know what goes on at school.

Communication

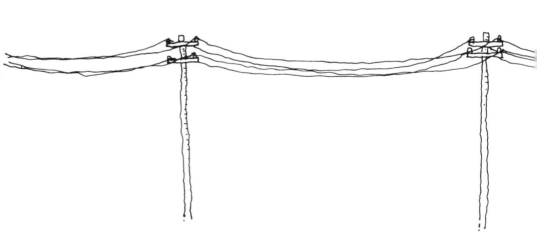

When I was still in broadcasting, hosting a talk show on the local CBS channel, I occasionally wanted to interview a teacher about a school event—a county band going to Europe, or a Christmas planetarium show open to the public, or an art exhibition featuring all the new Gold Key winners in the Scholastic Contest. There were many interesting topics in our high schools. I would call the school office and leave my carefully worded message for the teacher in charge of the event; I would leave my number and the hours when I would be available; I would even leave my home number. Rarely did the teacher ever call back. I found this very puzzling, until I became a teacher, ironically, a teacher of Speech Communication.

We had four phones at Bexley Hills High School for 1190 people. This was not counting the phone in the office of the Athletic Director, nor the phones in the principals' offices, nor the nurse's phone nor that of the Cafeteria Manager. In other words, five people had five phones and 1185 people had four phones. Plus one outdoor phone.

That outdoor phone was a real ringer, pun intended. I'd be scuttling along the cement porch on a 19-degree day, (it was half a block of traveling from "Bexley North" to the center of the building), when I'd hear the outdoor phone start to ring. It would ring and ring and ring. Some 9th grader from another school was calling his girlfriend (probably from his school's outdoor phone), and she meanwhile had forgotten about all the prior arrangement on this 10:17 phone call, or was in the clutch of a teacher because she had forgotten the day was Cycle 5, not Cycle 6 (that is, Tuesday and not Wednesday).

Communication

The phone went on ringing. This meant that I, a teacher, in desperate search of a phone, had better just fade on by. If the phone were not ringing, I could deposit my quarter, or be prepared with my Bell IQ card for a long distance call, and try to complete the call before the next bell. If the bell would ring first, I could shout, but I would not be able to hear and and/or–in the confusion amidst the horde of passing students I would drop all the notes and miscellany I was holding in my other hand.

Better perhaps to try the office phone, the extra one "reserved for teachers". At this phone four secretaries with oversize ears could monitor the call. When long distance calls were coming in for me, the cozy office phone was where I took them. This modern method of communication worked thusly:

In my classroom I would be buzzed on the intercom–"Mrs. Juditz, can you take a long distance phone call?" Quick thinking now. Was this a class that would or would not vandalize the room while I would be gone for five minutes...or would they disappear? A class of nine students did disappear one time when I took a long distance call. When I hung up I saw them all being herded into the Principal's office. Or was this a class that would not vandalize the room, nor disappear, but would chew each other up with sharp objects? Stones from the planter on the windowsill, bent paper clips, tacks from the bulletin board? Assuming it was a reasonable class, sleepy but harmless, I would say briskly, "Yes, I'll be right there!"

Then I would begin the long, high-heeled hike to the Office. Along the outer 19-degree porch, picking my way over the chewing tobacco blotches. Through the steel doors, then left past the Detention Room where several students waved a hand. Down the long dim hallway to the OFFICE, and the OFFICE PHONE. With a little luck I would have remembered to bring the correct folder, depending upon which speech contest was upcoming: the District League, the Voice of Democracy, the Civic Garden Club Environmental Broadcast Contest. If I had guessed wrong, I would have to promise to call back near the end of the day.

I remember on one January morning in the early 80's, the voice at the other end of the line was the Director of the Speech League, the woman whom I had replaced on the Bexley faculty when she accepted the League post at the State University.

She said, "0 thank God you're there...I was beginning to think they couldn't find you. And I have a big, big favor to ask..."

"Oh", I said, "and what is it?"

"I need you to run the Regional Drama Tournament this Saturday, down at Pennsworth in Bucks County. You'll have the place to yourself, and I already have a list of possible judges you can call–you'll need five. Just use your local trophy dealer. Ron Maugher was to have been in charge of the Regional Tournament ... he has a death in the family. I know you'll know exactly what to do...I can't think of anyone else who could do it half as effectively. And since your own school is not involved there'll be no extra problems for you."

By this time I was wishing I had stayed with my class or opted to call back at the end of the day. Most of all, I was wishing my own play had qualified at District level for Regional Competition. Useless to wish anything. There was no turning down Mrs. Grant. She didn't ask, she set you up. That's what a League Director was for. When she said you'd have the place to yourself, that meant it would take an extra half hour at seven on Saturday morning to find someone who would have a key to the school.

This was Tuesday morning. The contest was Saturday. I would have to call back to Mrs. Grant to work out details. The calls to judges would be to other schools with one phone for 400 persons. Even if I could get to a phone, the people I needed to reach were also teachers who could not get to THEIR phones. Only the trophy shop would be easy to reach. Once, in the mid-70's, there was a phone nstalled in the North Basement Book Room of Bexley, a few doors down from my classroom. After a few months, the chairman of the English Department made the recommen- dation that the phone be removed. And his recommenda- tion was honored! I didn't know why. His office was a full city block from that phone. Was he just being nasty? Since he couldn't have a phone to arrange parent conferences, invite guest speakers, schedule field trips, did he begrudge any- one else having a phone as close as thirty seconds away? It was true that a guidance secretary and a computer teacher met occasionally in the bookroom, but the chairman of the English Department was allegedly a happily married man with two small children and no designs on either the secretary or the teacher. WHAT WAS HIS MOTIVE????

For the next ten years I tried to have that phone rein-stalled–the jack was still there. I almost made it one year by going directly to the Chief Custodian, who told me he had a number of surplus phones. Alas, an assistant principal in charge of room improvements told the Chief these phones were not for use.

Eventually (the late 80's) there was one extra phone installed. In the Guidance Department. In a conference room. And this phone, the Administration let it be known, was for TEACHERS, to use sitting in the warm, comfortable conference room, in private, with the door closed, so that parent calls could be given top priority, etc, etc.

There were two problems, however: the conference room often had a conference in it (especially a psychologi-cal conference beginning at 7:15 am, with psychologist, six grim-faced teachers and two tight-lipped parents and a prin-cipal to EmCee. Or at day's end, sixteen minutes after class time, the door was locked by the guidance secretary, whose computer, word processor, coat rack and philodendron were already in darkness, she having prepared to leave by 3:02.

Early on in my teaching career I understood that at home, in the evening, on the week-end, Sunday morning even, was the time to do my professional phoning. And about four years after I retired I learned from an article in a state educational journal why there were no phones in class-rooms. The writer of the article stated, "More than 60 years ago Congress passed a law designed to facilitate home wiring for telephone service. The Universal Access Law excluded public-schools from its cost-saving measures, and every rewrite of the law in subsequent years continued to ignore public school classrooms until November 1996. The 1996 Telecommunications Act amends the 1934 law by providing federal funding to wire the public schools and guarantee a low phone rate. The goal is to achieve "connectivity."

"I did not reach Thee
But my feet slip nearer
every day..."

Emily Dickinson

Résumé

When I was in college I prepared to be a teacher. Many members of my family had been teachers: my grandmother, my grandfather, my mother, my aunts, my grand aunts and great uncles–all were teachers at one time or another.

My grandmother at age sixteen began to teach in a one-room-school house, Beaver Creek. She had 62 students, when they were all present. Fortunately, half were rarely present because they had to work at home; thus, she had a manageable group of about thirty students, from age 6 to 18. Many of the students could speak Pennsylvania Dutch only; most of the boys chewed tobacco (and often missed the spittoon.) Some of the children had no shoes, even in winter; a few were too poor to bring any lunch, even a lard sandwich. They shared the teacher's lunch. With her total annual earnings of $125.00, my grandmother bought an organ and a beautiful new hat. She taught for just two winters, then married and settled down to raise a family. She lived to be 91, and during the many years I knew her, she talked with more pride about her teaching than anything else she had ever done.

From age five, I had wished to be a teacher. When I graduated from college, however, there were no jobs available in my field: there were vacancies for gym teachers and math teachers–I was certified in English and French. Therefore, the day after graduation I went to work in a broadcasting station. My Speech professor in college had a friend of a friend who owned a radio station, and the copy girl was just leaving to get married.

Resume

I had never written any advertising copy; I didn't even know how to type. But the owner of the station, a soft-spoken, pipe-smoking gentleman-of-the-old-school, assured me that I could handle the copy, that I was sure to enjoy the program assignment–the chance to interview interesting leaders of the community and celebrities who might be passing by. My starting salary would be $50 per week–$35.00 from the station and $15.00 from talent fees (paid by sponsors).

At that time I did not know that only two persons in a small radio station ever made any money–the owner and the sales manager. There was no union, no wage scale, no benefits. But I had an office of my own and I loved the work. Well, I loved the ON AIR work. In two weeks I had taught myself to type, and soon I could grind out copy–hundreds of commercials, some with musical backgrounds, some with multi-characters (many played by me). I wrote special shows for Thanksgiving and Christmas, along with a series for Sunday evening called, "The Poet's Corner". The staff announcers, the program director, the receptionist, the bookkeeper–all these fellow workers were hungry for ON AIR assignments, too; it was no problem persuading them to be my actors.

I acquired a title: Women's Program Director. Had my own talk show and another weekly program called, "Your Doctor Speaking", where I interviewed local physicians on subjects such as "ectopic pregnancy", "osteomyelitis", "neurological disorders". I was not particularly interested in medical topics, but my fifteen-dollar-per-week-talent-fee, paid by the local Medical Society, was good enough reason in 1950 to be interested in flu symptoms.

I stayed at that little 250-watt station for eight years. Once I was given a $2.00 per week raise. This was such a humiliating experience that on my next lunch break I hunted out the City Education Department (it was located in a downtown alley), and picked up an application for a teaching assignment. The secretary recorded my name, address and phone number and then said, "When you fill out the application you'll note that the form says, married women are not eligible to teach in the District. However there has been some change in policy, so perhaps that does not always apply...".

Well, I was married. I couldn't fathom why they wouldn't want a MARRIED female teacher. The District office wasn't reassuring either: green window shades, dust on the sills, streaked and unwashed windows, floors badly in need of sanding or at least covering up. When I returned to the Studio at the end of lunch hour, a memo was waiting. I was to interview Bob Hope, soon to be in town for the world premiere of "The Seven Little Foys". I forgot all about the teaching job application.

Finally, I did leave that station to move with my husband and year-old daughter to Columbus, Ohio. Bob was in charge of launching a new branch for his insurance company. In our Columbus garden apartment we soon became friends with the couple who lived upstairs; the husband was a personnel manager for a TV station. I launched my TV career at WTVN Columbus.

As a TV spokeswoman I sold picnic supplies on shows such as "Sergeant Preston of the Yukon". My daughter, who was just learning to talk, began to imitate me; in her bubble bath water she would hold up a duck or plastic boat, and as she showed it off at various angles, a large smile would break over her face.

The pay for TV commercials was double radio fees. More importantly, I learned the value of the union: I could not even touch a refrigerator door—a props man assigned only to refrigerators opened that door for me on cue. I was allowed to work for two weeks outside the union, and then I was required to join, at a rate much kinder than had I been, let's say in New York, Chicago, or even Philadelphia. I was now a card-carrying member of AFTRA, American Federation of Television and Radio Artists.

The Columbus Career was short-lived, however. We missed our families and friends, so when the chance came for Bob to take the branch division back to the Central Region, I finished my last refrigerator commercial, and in one of the snowiest winters on record, we moved back east. And into a decade of what would surely be remembered as one of the most significant in U.S. history—the 1960's.

Again I lucked out. A local CBS affiliate talk-show hostess was just leaving to have a baby, to join a husband who had been transferred. I auditioned, I was chosen to replace her. I had an office and a FULL HOUR OF SHOW TIME. There were interviews with local politicians, Junior League officers, visiting celebrities, like Lassie and Harold Stassen, the-man-who-would-be-President, along with our

State Lt. Governor, the-man-who-fervently-hoped-to-be-Governor. Eventually I had a live audience and a piano player all my own.

There were bridal shows and Christmas toy shows, contests to judge, Inaugural Balls to attend, passes to everywhere. And once in a while, it was possible to put together a show that counted.

Staff members of the State Museum brought us artifacts of Native Americans; feathers and fins from natural history in our river valley, and introductions to the antiquities of pewter, porcelain and hand-crafted furniture. The city's Foreign Policy Association organized Great Decisions discussions. My daughter's First Grade teacher accepted my invitation to have the entire class visit the show as a field trip; surely it was educational–Ralph Smedley of Toastmasters International was also there that day to share in the conversation. At Christmas time during my third season as "Central PA's favorite talk-show hostess," I staged an informal TV party with high school seniors. Black and white high school seniors. And we talked about college and career plans. This was the first time black persons had ever appeared on local TV in any role other than entertainer–dancing, singing, playing a musical instrument, playing a game.

There was no dearth of interesting subjects–people, places, problems. The show was one hour, the preparation for it was 12 hours or so per day, mostly at home on the phone. This was live TV, this was low budget TV, this was public service TV. It was not until 1325 interviews and six years of show production later that I decided to retire from this career.

I did not "retire" because hours were long and financial pickings were meager. From the start I knew they would be meager. There was a union, the International Brotherhood of Electrical Workers. IBEW, as the name implied, was beholden to cable pullers, electricians, sound men, lighting technicians. They were not interested in "talent". I was on that fringe known as "talent".

No, the real reason was—the winds of change were gaining momentum in broadcasting. The winds of change were snuffing out public service time: time for museums, time for schools, time for debate on controversial subjects. In the newsroom appeared a note pinned to the bulletin board: INTERVIEWS HAVING TO DO WITH COMMUNITY RACIAL TENSIONS ARE NOT TO BE SCHEDULED.

I had two weeks' notice that my show was being dropped. I was to continue to tape some radio commentary (a 10-minute public service segment); I was also invited, nay ENCOURAGED, to telecast the 11 pm Weather.

After agreeing to continue the radio public service feature, I decided the time had come to take up the teaching profession. I started small—as a substitute—to help out—this was in the autumn of 1966. Then suddenly, the Speech teacher for whom I was substituting was called away to be the Director of the Speech League at the State University. It all happened so quickly the District Superintendent hired me without even asking that I take a loyalty oath; (the McCarthy Era still lingered on in our region even though the senator had died more than ten years earlier), nor did I have to appear before the School Board of the South Shore District.

Actually, I knew the wife of the Superintendent. A singer, she had appeared on my TV show to promote her singing group. She loved my show; she loved to appear on it, and her husband, Superintendent of the South Shore School District, of which Bexley Hills High was the crown jewel, was of that traditional philosophy, "If the Wife says it's good, it's good". I was hired. At $5400 per annum, two hundred dollars more than state law decreed they would have to pay a beginning teacher.

Thus, on a snowy, bitterly cold day, December 19, 1966, I came to Bexley Hills High School, a passionate descendent of teachers, with a love for teaching. I arrived as a professional with 20 years' experience in the marketplace of my subject. This, you realize, was before we were called "educators", "learning facilitators", or even "teachers". We were "school teachers". Our union was SSEA–South Shore Education Association, and it cost $15.00 to belong.

"...first thing to do is to fall
in love with your work..."

NINE STEPS TO SUCCESS
-Sister Lauretta

Home Room Period

In 1966 the school day began at 8:15 with a homeroom period. Bible reading and prayer had faded with the 50's, but the "Home Room Period" lingered on. There were announcements over the PA, an inspirational reading, many of which were taken from a ten-pound anthology titled "The School Day Begins". The reading was followed by a few moments for meditation.

During the homeroom period there was time to make up a test, deliver messages, receive messages, take a vocab quiz, buy tickets in the office for whatever event was upcoming, call home, for forgotten items–a gym suit, an art project. The homeroom period was a time for collections: Budget collection (paying ahead for tickets to sports events, concerts, the Yearbook), United Fund collection, class dues collection. And it was the time for picture taking: ALL DEBATERS REPORT TO THE LOBBY!

In time, those teachers who were wont to complain the loudest at faculty meetings whined that the home room period was a waste of time, a situation where it was very difficult to keep order and good discipline. They, of course, were not the teachers who had to organize collections, give make-up, and vocab quizzes, schedule yearbook pictures; they were not even the teachers who could hear morning readings and maintain a few moments for silent meditation. They were teachers who did not even have home rooms. They were the Gym teachers and sports coaches and trainers, who found those 43 minutes of non-practice an abomination.

First there was a compromise: the homeroom period was switched to the END of the day. Students who had sports and co-curricular programs, such as band, chorus, drama, could now be excused from homeroom. At that point order and discipline did become a problem for home room teachers because the only students left in home room were the squirmy, squirrelly NON-students who had no activities, who were majoring in hall walking and bathroom smoking (smoking in the lavs–the Principal always said LABS, but the rest of us knew what was accurate).

Finally, the home room period was phased out. Collections, vocab quizzes, message exchange, ticket buying could now be done in NINE minutes, right after the inspirational reading and the 15 seconds for meditation, with the very abbreviated announcements read rather breathlessly by the quickest available principal.

By the time the 80's arrived the school day was beginning at 7:45, ending at 2:45; Seniors with honor passes could leave at 2:15, if they had a last-period study hall. The yellow buses began pulling in at 2:10 and were kept running until 2:45, their billowing exhaust fumes commingling with the belching sulphur effluvium of the chem labs.

Soon there were frequent teacher-parent conferences at 7 am, with or without a psychologist present, with or without a principal to EmCee. The morning reading had also undergone a metamorphosis: it had become the Star Spangled Banner, sometimes sung by Aretha Franklin, sometimes by Robert Goulet, sometimes by the Bexley Hills Chamber Singers, and once in awhile by a squealy, unrec-

ognizable trio. There was no meditation, and the announcements were now brought to all rooms in printed form. At the
top of the page was the day's list of Early Dismissals,
Detention Sitters, and Out-of-School-Suspension-Servers.

Then came TV. CHANNEL ONE, THE HIGH
SCHOOL PEER TV. Channel One had been trying for three
years to break into Bexley Hills. Finally, the offer of a FREE
TV SET IN EVERY ROOM and "ten minutes of truly worth-
while news broadcast by high school students from across
the nation" did it. The vote at the May 1992 Faculty Meeting
won for TV.

It was surely not to our professional credit that no
one stood up in that meeting to point out that already the
average person in the U.S. was watching TV 30 hours a
week, or that TV at its best was a waste of time because of
what else the students were NOT doing—music lessons,
games, clubs, coherent conversation, or that the real reason Channel One wanted to be at Bexley was to sell Pepsi,
pizza, and acne preparations. THE SCHOOL DAY, it was
now decreed, WOULD BEGIN WITH TV!

In one sense, "home room" had returned, for this TV
audience was not to be the Period One class members, but
the students assigned to the teacher from whom they
picked up report cards four times a year.

In my home room of 27 students, whose names all
began with the letter "F", about 14 watched Channel One
without comment; the other 13 began to fidget and talk. One
surly boy would mutter as I passed his desk (hoping to keep
him quiet by my presence), "Look Old Lady, bug off. I don't

need you, I don't want you".

In all fairness to Channel One, the news items were covered accurately and sometimes in-depth, the student announcers were capable, cheerful communicators, and at 7:30 in the morning the commercials for candy bars, sodas, and pizza somehow seemed more innocuous than if they had been run, let's say, at 11 am or 2 pm.

My aunt, who had taught in a city high school from 1929 to 1965, used to say that Bible reading did settle everyone down and the day could get organized in a civilized way. Inspirational readings, of which I was in charge at Bexley for about a dozen years, had somewhat the same effect. Occasionally someone would even request a copy of a selection that had been read.

As I stood guard over my students watching Channel One, I remembered my own high school home room of the 1940's: a girls' home room, where we had planned programs at least twice a week poetry readings, story telling, flower arranging, birthday celebrations. We elected officers, learned parliamentary procedure, held informal debates. For many years after graduation we would hold reunions, and at the time, of our 50th School Reunion, there were still several of us who kept in touch with the lady who had been our homeroom teacher.

Dr. William Glasser, in his book, "Schools Without Failure" wrote: "Solving the problem of impersonality in secondary schools is not easy. One suggestion that I believe has merit is to increase the use of the home room... the home room can, given more time, also be used for social-problem-solving and open ended class meetings...students and teachers will get to know each other better."

"Last year we said, 'Things,
can't go on like this',
and they didn't, they got worse."

                    -Will Rogers

The Spoken Word

There actually was a textbook called, "The Spoken Word". Not to be confused with a religious treatise, nor the popular poetry anthology; it was a skinny, cheaply bound text chosen for a one-semester speech course. Maybe the smarter and not-nice students caught on quickly about the "cheaply bound" quality: they decimated those books, filled them with obscene writing and pictures, vandalized the covers, mutilated the spines. All the desecration against the English language, normally scratched on lavatory walls, found its way into those unassuming little books.

But this all happened in the mid-80's. It was in the Spring of 1972 that I had my first real battle with "obscenity".

Dr. Horace Hennings, a slightly built, rusty-haired, wrinkle-faced man, was the Superintendent. Mr. James Anderson, always described as "a big man with a big heart", was the Principal of Bexley Hills, and the Assistant Principal was Mr. Arthur Zimmerman.

Mr. Zimmerman had a problem with "nerves", was on a valium prescription; in conferences Mr. Zimmerman would always nod pleasantly, speak rarely and remember nothing. I was listed as Advisor of Thespian Troupe 1282. We four had a conference on May 31, 1972, the day after Memorial Day. It was indeed a memorable day.

Mr. Anderson drove me to the Administration Office. On the way there I thought, well! This is it. Exactly what those articles were about in DRAMATICS magazine, the official Thespian Troupe publication. Articles about school administrators objecting to play subjects, the language of the script, sometimes the costume of a character. I had always felt so thankful after reading that material, because I had never been challenged, no one had ever asked for "prior approval", no one had ever put together a list of "acceptable plays".

In Dr. Hennings' air-conditioned office, my palms were sweaty; I sat a bit straighter in my chair; my teeth were tight together. The play in question was from "America Hurrah", by world-famous playwright Jean vanItalie. Our Repertory Theatre players of the Thespian Troupe had just presented the play at the City Arts Festival during the past week-end. I heard Dr. Hennings' voice saying that although he had not seen the play he had had several calls about the language of the play.

I thought back to what I had deleted from the script–"mother fucker" was one among several–I thought this might be out of line for the community audience. (Probably it wasn't, but I was trying to be politically correct twenty years ahead of time.)

As the conference continued, I doubted that SEV-ERAL calls had been received by Dr. Hennings. From pre-vious experience about complaints in general, the remarks to a teacher were always prefaced with "we have had sev-eral complaints". Actually one person, usually a friend of the administrator, was the "several complaints". Someone had called. This someone had taken her small child to the festi-val at 8:30 in the evening, and this was what the child had seen and heard. Dr. Hennings explained all this to me in the conference, while Mr. Anderson was fidgeting in his chair and Mr. Zimmerman's eyelids were almost shut. Dr.

Hennings concluded his remarks with, "Mrs. Juditz, I'm very sorry all this has happened. Your Children's Theatre plays have always been received very warmly."

I bit my tongue. I thought it too cheeky to point out that this was not a Children's Theatre play–it had not been billed as such. Plays at 8:30 in the evening on a downtown festival stage are not for children unless clearly advertised as such, and that would be most unusual.

My silent rebuttal went racing on–Dr. Hennings, you're such an idiot. You've never been to the Arts Festival downtown, you're probably afraid to go downtown. And you certainly don't know anything about theatre. Repertory or otherwise. You never show up for our main stage plays. If you really want to check on obscenity and all kinds of up-to-the-moment street language, why don't you stroll the halls of Bexley?

The next morning I received a copy of the Conference Minutes: "The Superintendent received several telephone calls complaining about obscenities in the play presented by Bexley Hills Thespian Troupe at the City Arts Festival, May 27, 1972. Conference was devoted to discussion of how play was selected, role of Advisor and of Building Principal. It was established that the play did contain vulgar and obscene comments and that several of these comments were removed from the script by Mrs. Juditz. However, several were permitted to remain in the script including the words "goddamn", "bastard", and "hooker". As a result of this conference the Advisor to the Thespians, Mrs. Juditz, was directed to exercise more control over the selection of plays and to make them conform to the mores and standards of this community. It was further directed that the building principal, Mr. Anderson, was to be consulted and involved in the choice of presentations before they were prepared for public showing."

In the student handbook of the 70's there had been no mention of school policy about obscenity, foul language, about what punishment would result when a student cursed a teacher or another student. The student handbook, issued to every student at the start of the school year, had many pages about sports, clubs, dates when report cards would be issued, dates for holidays, which radio station carried snow-day information.

By the mid-80's the TEACHER'S handbook had a lot to say about bad language: reprimand, report to office, fill out Incident Report–very little of this was practical to do, given the number of times offensive language occurred during the day. Quite true that the language had become appalling–among the students, among the teachers, and sometimes students to teachers. (As a rule the teacher did not use bad language to a student). "Old Lady", "Mrs. Uterus", "Jew Lady", and the usual street expletives were all spun off to me at one time or another.

But the most unexpected, most outrageous example of spoken-word misbehavior came from Enid, a brown-haired, fairly attractive 9th grader. I had finished giving instructions for the day's writing assignment: "Write about your home town", and I had listed a few sub-topics–the people, the stores, places to go for entertainment, etc, etc. Enid looked me straight in the eye and said, "You know what you are Mrs. Juditz? You are a big TURD."

I wanted to laugh, but I didn't. I also wanted to say, "Shut the hell up, Enid, and get to the writing."

I didn't. I said, in the proscribed Teacher's Handbook voice, "You are being very rude, Enid. Please begin your writing, write to the end of the period, when it will be time to hand in your paper."

With two hours of play rehearsal ahead, one hour of phone calls later in the evening to parents, and a nightcap of written work to evaluate, I had no spare time to fill out an Incident Report. Probably the Assistant Principal who always said, "I have at least 30 reports a day", would be grateful.

The Student's Handbook now had pages and pages of rules relating to spoken-word-behavior and official school policy thereof. Obviously fear was escalating in the administration about the power of the spoken word. Yet now, just as back in Dr. Hennings' day, the only place to control language would be in a school play. How ironic, since a play serves as a mirror of society and helps us see our faults.

You will recall that the first incident of this chapter, the one about the festival play, occurred in 1972. It was six years later that the following directive came down from the administrative office. There was now a new Superintendent, an extra Assistant Super and a new Building Principal. The date, July 12, 1978. The extra Assistant Super wrote:

The Spoken Word

*I don't know how much you become involved
when dramas to be presented at various
times during the school term in your
building are selected. If you have not
touched base with your drama coaches lately
about the selection, you ought to be
thinking about it.*

*The tenor of the times certainly allows
broader interpretation on TV, the stage,
and in motion pictures than at any other
time in our history. This coupled with the
sexual maturity of our students and the
rather free spirits that drama coaches usually are, magnifies the problem.*

*The kind of presentation an avant-garde
coach or group of students may be pushing,
especially in the shorter and one-act off
Broadway variety, is generally not the kind
of play our people in general would appreciate. Even though some would go to New
York or Philadelphia or our own community
theatre to see them, does not in any way
guarantee acceptance.*

*Changing mores does not always have to
mean changing values. Our kids have a
rough time understanding, accepting, and*

*keeping values as it is. When we as a
scheel contribute te the confusien, Ged
knews what we de te their thinking. If yeu
haven't dene se up till new, please get
invelved in seme way in the dramatics
selectiens at yeur scheel. I persenally
den't recemmend that yeu serve as the
final CENSOR. It puts yeu in a teugh spet
that yeu den't need. I de recemmend, hew-
ever, that yeu establish a staff/student
cemmittee chaired by yeu, er a reliable
appeintee, te review and select presenta-
tiens fer yeur scheel.*

Dr. Norman Samuels was now Principal. It is to his everlasting credit that, to my knowledge, no such committee or reliable person was ever appointed. He was one of the few principals who came to every show, with his wife, stayed for the full length of the show, and wrote a short note to me afterwards, saying how much they had enjoyed the performance. The writer of the drama memo faded from the scene. I have no idea whatever happened to him. In his own language God knows whatever happened to him.

"On a good day, good words
must be spoken"

-Ovid

The Ten O'Clock Scholar

Speech contests were a mid-winter activity. Speech contestants were mostly honor students, often theater students as well. I served as their coach, their chaperone, their keeper of the kleenex, petty cash for the phone, and tickets for lunch. Very often, I was their driver.

For my first contest in that winter of 1967 our host school was a nearby parochial institution. I had everybody properly registered way ahead of time, by mail; all entry fees had been paid; every contestant was well-prepared, with Parental Permission slip signed, including the senior boy whose topic in Persuasive Division was, "Homosexuals: a Plea for Equality". The coach whom I was replacing on the faculty staff had told me, "Bert's speech is actually all ready. He's wel1-researched, well-rehearsed". She didn't add whether or not he spoke from personal experience. I was never to know that–it was going to be ten more years before the son of a magazine editor got up to speak in my honors class and started his speech with, "I'm gay and glad of it".

In any event, I was prepared and put together for that first big contest of the season. I set out with a carful of contestants, and we were just one block from the host school, at a busy intersection, when suddenly the car died. Just DIED. This had never happened to me before. Whatever else we did or didn't do in our family, whatever our shortcomings, our cars were always in tip top shape.

"You know something, Mrs. J.?"

"What, Debbie?" Debbie was in Extemporaneous Speaking Division.

"I think you're out of gas. Look at the dial."

I looked. I was. Totally on "E". However, I was stalled opposite a service station, With cars lining up in back of me and car drivers scowling, and a few on the horn, I managed to get an attendant (all stations were full serve in those days) to bring a can of gas, get the car into the service island, gas up, AND WE WERE STILL ON TIME: no penalty for late arrival.

If my coaching image was tarnished, my contestants were kind enough not to make any comment. All other memories of that day are gone, but surely the pattern must have been much like that of other contests that followed in rapid succession.

Many speech contests were held on week-ends, sometimes beginning on Friday evening at five (such as the fateful first one) and running until about 10 pm. Then up and out early on Saturday morning for an eight o'clock round. There would be about a hundred and fifty contestants from thirty-six different schools; each contestant had to participate in at least three rounds, meeting three different judges. Then the top-ranking students would enter semi-final rounds. And the highest-ranking of those competitors would eventully be in the FINAL ROUND, where there would be FIVE JUDGES, and every available seat in the room would be-filled with anxious parents, loyal friends, and other curious contestants who had dropped by the wayside earlier in the day. Highlight of the contest was the Awards Assembly, with its glittering trophies in three different sizes and the snowy piles of certificates, hand-lettered. Awards assemblies would begin as late as half-past eight on Saturday

evening. Since contestants were very reliable, very dedi-
cated in the 60's and 70's, this ambitious schedule was no
problem. Except for an occasional, unusual, nay, unique,
contestant. Hank Nace, for example.

Hank was not an "A" student. Hank was not a student at all. He was enrolled at the school, he attended
classes, but I don't recall that he ever carried books, wrote
papers, or burdened himself with notebook, pen, or pencil.
Somehow he was managing a passing average. So why did
I have him in contests? Two reasons: he had an unusual
tone in his voice–like a carnival guy, who had such reso-
nance, such silky slyness–as a listener you were drawn in,
and you knew you were being drawn in, but it was fascinating all the same; and Hank loved poetry–Poetry Reading
was a very prestigious division of the contests. Actually,
there was a third reason. Hank was a free spirit; he looked
the role and he looked like the poems he loved–the ones
from "Coney Island of the Mind", by Lawrence Ferlinghetti.
Many mornings when I was driving to school, I would see
Hank swinging along in his fringed, brown suede jacket, his
chestnut hair–shoulder length or more–waving behind him.

The school administration did not like Hank's hair. At
the time Hank was in school, there were 26 other males who
had shoulder length (or longer) hair. Hair became such a sensitive issue that Hank was about to be barred from any and
all contests, if he persisted in having shoulder length hair.

"Hank Nace must not represent Bexley Hills High
School in shoulder length hair!", the Principal told me.

He didn't. He did compete, but he didn't appear in

shoulder length hair. We took along a wig in a little wig box, and before registration time Hank donned his wig in the boys' lav, and he wore his wig all the hours of the contest. If he were not quite as Coney-Island-of-the-Mind looking, he still sounded the same, and he scored just as well.

Hank also appeared in the first full-length play I directed for the school–"Up the Down Staircase", based on the book by Belle Kauffman. And yes, he played the part of the student who hated school and wanted to quit.

What I really wanted to tell you about Hank in the first place was that getting him to contests involved a certain strategy. Hank liked to sleep late. He lived with his Dad and sister; Dad was often away, the sister was not an early riser, either. I would give Hank a wake-up call, sometimes TWO wake-up calls, give him enough time to get into the fringed outfit, then stop by his house to pick him up. (The rule was, students reported to the school and I picked them up there. Hank could not be counted on to get these rules straight).

Eventually Hank satisfied the requirements for graduation, and I helped him–no, really I wrote FOR him–his letter of application to the American Academy of Dramatic Arts in New York City, and I added a letter of recommendation.

It was seventeen years later that I thoroughly enjoyed his performance as the Emperor in "Amadeus" at our Community Theater. This is what I read in the Who's Who of the program:

"Hank Nace last appeared in our theater during the 79-80 season, when he acted as Fred in "Scrooge" and as Dr. Chumley in "Harvey". Earlier he had been in "A Midsummer Night's Dream (Demetrius)". He was educated at Penn State University. Professionally, he directed Harold Pinter's, "The Collection", at the Circle Theater in New York and played James in the production. He has worked in the summer stock programs at the area college and was the Resident Director of the Commonwealth Stage Company, where he developed the Children's Theatre Department and taught acting workshops. Hank has done television and radio commercials in New York and South Central PA. After being away from acting and directing for five years he says he "recently got the urge to go back to it".

As Emperor Joseph II, Hank still had the unusual tone in his voice, he obviously loved his role, and his almost shoulder length wig looked especially appropriate, too.

Driving home after the play that evening, the thought occurred to me that most people on the outside of school probably have no idea what a speech coach is. My own college, when updating its alumni roster had sent me a form. I duly reported my profession: Speech Educator and Coach.

At the close of the next season the alumni office sent me a request for patron status in the Basketball Boosters Club.

I believe there is nothing more important than coaching for skills that will last a lifetime. Seventeen years from now Hank is likely to turn up in a role at age sixty or so "because he just felt like getting back to it again".

A diller, a dollar
A ten o'clock scholar.
What makes you come so soon?
You used to come at 10 o'clock
And now you come at noon!"

-Nursery Rhyme

The Actor Takes Pain

Interesting point—Hank Nace working on Pinter's "Collection". Our work on this play had pre-dated Hank's tenure at Bexley by about eight years.

To be candid, I knew very little about competitive theatre when I signed my school contract in December of 1966. I knew college theatre, community theatre, In-House Company Theatre FUN (the kind of show I had directed for my husband's company), summer stock theatre, church pageants, High School Junior and Senior plays. But "competitive theatre", other than a hazy memory about the Greek one-act plays presented for prizes, had not been part of my acting experience. Competitive high school theatre had slipped into the co-curricular programs sometime in the 50's, along side Debate and Speech Contests, the latter two known as "forensics" before WWII.

I had had personal experience with forensics before WWII: the fact that I had been bested by an ash blond boy from McKeesport, PA in Shakespearean Reading could still bring a twinge of resentment.

In the file of "Suggested Titles" left for me by Mrs. Grant, the faculty coach who was my predecessor, the top choice for one-act-plays-competitive, was "The Collection" by Harold Pinter. I was sure Mrs. Grant had left the list to start me off in the direction to win, place, or show in any play contest or festival we might enter. She had been seven years at Bexley, had put many of the League rules in place herself, had established an enviable reputation in Communication for the school. Now, as Director of the League, she was not expecting to be embarrassed by mistakes of the coach from her former school; she expected me to keep the program in place—the Speech Contests, the Drama Club with its Repertory Theatre events, Children's Theatre, two full-length annual plays, Choral Reading for holiday assemblies, and especially significant, the COM-PETITIVE THEATER which she had recently founded for the League.

In the publisher's catalogue I noted the following information about "The Collection": this intriguing short play probes into the tensions and conflicts which surround four people who seek to learn the unfortunate truth about each other... all this is done with subtlety and good taste and affords a stimulating glimpse into the shadow abyss that lies between the true and the false, illusion and reality..."

Keeping in mind that this was our once-a-year opportunity to perform a controversial, uncensored and thought-provoking piece, "The Collection" seemed to be a wise choice for the 1968 competition play. The contest rules were precise: time length-20 to 40 minutes; number of char-acters-at least three; scenery-very minimal; costumes-no extra credit given for fine costuming-costuming should sim-ply be "appropriate"; hand-props-simple, appropriate, con-sistant; no musicals allowed, no first place winning script from previous year allowed; must be a one-act or a cutting from a longer play.

Again, "The Collection" qualified on all counts. Next question: did I have on hand the four actors—three males and a female—who could handle this play? Who would appreciate a serious theme? Who could do justice to

Pinter's talent for mysterious menace in a "stunning and frightening one-act play"? (as the publisher's description continued). AND, maybe even more to the point, did I have four actors who would be consistent with their English accents? I was convinced I did.

There was tremendous advantage in having a co-curricular speech program with three different levels: the basic public speaking course, the next level in broadcasting and debate, the third gradation in theatre and discussion. All were elective courses at that time, classes at the two upper levels were small; I already knew who could handle accents, create a believable character, who had forty hours of time to put a competition play together.

We would use "The Collection" for play festival work as well, and because our most prestigious annual festival was now being held in a barn, with audience on three sides, we would gain the added experience of adjusting the set. Low-cut furniture would be created from some of our children's theatre lightweight boxes, draped and pillowed to become a contemporary London flat.

The first rehearsal, the read-through would give an accurate enough timing, along with a fair notion as to the pace required to sustain the mood. The following three rehearsals would be the tedium of blocking for a three-sided audience, thinking always how long dare I have the judge looking at the back of my head. Two rehearsals later, the lines would be memorized, not thoroughly, but well enough to allow the players to begin interpreting the role, to begin listening and reacting to the other players. Every time an actor goes over a scene at home or in rehearsal, he reminds himself of the kind of person his character is. How does he feel about the situation on each scene? What does he contribute to it, and how is he changed by it?

Now we are in the third week of rehearsal. The thrown-together mod furniture is working well—Pam Martin's mother has even offered a wicker chaise, very low-cut (and surely more comfortable than the unyielding wooden boxes). It is time to think about costumes, time to make lists of the real hand-props to be used—substitute dishes, flowers, phones must soon be scrapped. There are also lighting and sound plots to be drawn up, paper work to be completed on requisitioning a van, special meetings to be scheduled for crew members.

You will perhaps recall that "The Collection" has, in addition to the four players, a CAT. A cat very important to the mood of the play. My cat in 1968 was Smokey Marble—a beautiful, carefully bred American shorthair. She was an Allenwood cat (that means bred in one of our better suburbs); her eyes were large and topaz, hence her name to express smokey marbles. She was not a stage cat, but she learned quickly, and she liked Pam Martin, the girl who played Stella and had to hold CAT for long, thoughtful moments. (You will remember how many pregnant pauses there are in a Pinter play.) Smokey would join us for the last ten hours of rehearsal. This time would include the Technical Rehearsal (special drill on lights and sound) and the two Dress Rehearsals.

Our play festival in the early Spring of '68 was to be held at the Timbers Ranch, a dance camp about 15 miles from school. One traveled up dale and down, along green pastures, winding through woods thick with dogwood and red-bud trees, to a pristine natural setting with the stage in the center of a rustic barn. The audience sat on three sides of what once had been the haymow of the barn. I remember that day was so spring PERFECT, all sunshine and lightness. Surely a trophy-winning day!

We arrive at the Festival, two hours before performance time, have our time-allotted (twenty minutes) technical rehearsal. We are organized, VERY WELL ORGANIZED: all props in place, the low cut furniture quickly arranged, all floor taping carefully executed. The play begins, with timing very satisfactory; all actors are perfectly in character. The student cast as Bill, the young dress designer, in competitive theatre for the first time, is exceptionally effective in his role. And all four actors are great at their English accents.

As I said, the play was starting off extremely well. Only Smokey was having a bit of trouble. Far up in the barn rafters there were b i r d s.... She suddenly became aware of these.

As if responding to the Call of the Hunt, she took a flying- leap from Pam's lap, ran to the edge of the wooden stage floor and disappeared into the outer limits of the barn space.

My actors never stepped out of character, never missed a beat nor a pregnant pause. They continued smoothly to the end if the piece, well within the 40 minutes time period, with or without Cat. I was so proud of them; I expected them to be easily in Place or Show, maybe even WIN. The other plays did not seem particularly threatening–some unknowns and some too well-knowns.

After the plays, the judges retired for consultation. Finally they returned, ready to begin the oral critique. (Still no sign of Smokey Marble. No sound of the birds, either. Time to worry about that after the awards).

The Judge with the Blonde Hair was first. About our play she said in effect: "One cannot deny that the casting was carefully done for this play of mature theme." (Uh oh ... a judge talking about mature theme" was to mean trouble, always. It meant that the judge did not feel this was a subject appropriate for a high school play festival.) "And while all actors seemed to create their roles exceptionally well, it should perhaps be noted that for an actor less effort is required if one is just naturally correct for that role."

THAT BLONDE SHE-DEVIL! Assuming my actor "Bill the Young Dress Designer" was gay, assuming he was type-cast, assuming... She was from the Academy of Dramatic Arts in New York City, and although I have had to recommend a number of students for the school, I never held the place in high esteem after hearing the critique of that instructor.

No, we did not win a trophy. We had a rating of Excellent and were in fourth place. The winners were an adaptation of "Feathertop" (First Place), a cutting from "Fumed Oak" (Second), "The Bald Soprano" (Third); the latter two with no attempt at authentic accent. Certainly the writing quality of Hawthorn (albeit not a playwright), Coward and Ionesco deserves respect. Surely all three scripts were safe—"delightful fantasy", "comedy" and "hilarious comedy". We received a Special Judges' Commendation for Teamwork. I'm not sure this did much to mollify the disappointed feelings of the actors, who knew they were good, that the-script was excellent playwriting, that they had learned, especially with Smokey, the necessity for self-discipline, for solid concentration.

After a half-hour search we found Smokey Marble, her eyes still glued to the barn rafters. The birds had long flown. As always on the return trip from a contest, we discussed the performance.

Bill, the dress designer, had the first question.

"'Mrs. J., I just don't get it. If the casting was so good, and we were all so right for the parts, what was the blonde lady's problem?"

In real life, Bill was Mark Hemple, a junior science student, with a 99% average in Advanced Physics, I had to make sure that whatever answer I gave, Mark would not be too discouraged to try another festival.

"Mark, I'm not positive, but I think the lady's problem was that she didn't like the subject of the play. She'd rather be amused than asked to think about a serious conflict...unfortunately that prejudice influenced her judging."

"But that's not fair!" this from Pam who played Stella, "And anyway she's a theatre PROFESSOR. She shouldn't be subjective". The still small Voice of Mrs. Grant was in the back of my mind: " one of the hardest moments you'll face is how to explain a judge's decision to the students ", she had said. She was so right. Even in the short time I'd been at Bexley I had already learned that a high school contest play is unlike any other piece of theatre experience. The audience dare not applaud, there are cutting oral critiques, there are even more unkind WRITTEN critiques. If there are three judges, one will give you an excellent, another a good, and a third-fair. If there are five judges, you can get one superior, one excellent, one good, one fair, one poor. I have seen that happen! And if you have ONE JUDGE, God help you.

But for all the idiosyncrasies of these contests–the ironic unfairness, the grueling misery of hauling props and costumes and actors and stage crew, lighting and sound equipment, and in the case of a cutting from "Of Mice and Men", two big bales of hay for every performance–there is one wonderful point: since the function of theatre is to be the mirror of society, that is exactly what the well-knit play does. Holds up the mirror for us to see ourselves. Which fact is doubtless why there is so much disparity among the judges. It's a tough business to look into that mirror and admit the truth.

"We will meet and there we may
rehearse most obscenely and courageously.
Take pains, be perfect."

-A Midsummer Night's Dream

Class A Lunch

A School day begins as early as 7:10 am. And it can end as late as 11 pm, when the security system is reactivated, and it is assumed all humans have left the building.

It is possible to stay within the confines of the building during all of this time and be reasonably well-fed. There are vending machines in the school's main lobby, dispensing fifty choices of snacks, beverages, sunflower seeds, low-cal crackers, chips with various ethnic flavors, apples, oranges, pretzels, candies, sweet rolls, tiny pies.

Here is the Cafeteria, with a salad bar, a line for National Class A Type Lunch sample: Monday, October 8) Chuck-wagon Steak on Roll, Tri Tater, Buttered Carrots, Ice Cream, choice of white or chocolate milk. There is a soup and pizza line; there is a hamburger, hot dog, steak roll line.

In the Teachers' Lounge (a partly remodeled former furnace room) there are vending machines, a Microwave for those who have brought brown bag goodies that need microwaving and for those who make large quantities of popcorn. There is always a birthday cake to be shared, as well as a special table of desserts and snacks (for the fundraising benefit of some local group), such as home-made peanut butter eggs at Easter. On the door of the Teachers' Lounge is a large sign stating: STUDENTS, KNOCK AND WAIT.

All through the day there are students selling chocolate bars or taking orders for hoagies (or delivering the orders they have taken the week before); selling and ordering are not permitted IN CLASS, but expeditious ordering /selling goes on during the four minutes BETWEEN classes.

Aside from the sports events' concessions after hours, concerts and plays have snack tables. The annual Musical has a very nicely set up dessert cafe. Election Days in May and November bring food to the planetarium wing of the school, where not only does the citizenry of the 8th precinct vote, but the school debaters also earn a couple of hundred dollars with delicious homemade-sticky buns, donuts, juice, coffee.

About fifteen years ago, an edict came down from somewhere on high in the State Government that all vending machines had to be closed down during the regular lunch hours, the rationale being that if all fifty goodies were sealed up tightly so that no students could get to them, said students would HAVE TO EAT THE CLASS A LUNCH: meat and cheese sandwich, potato chips, carrot sticks, a banana, and choice of white or chocolate milk. This mandate was in the days before the salad bar, pizza and soup line, hamburger/hot dog choices.

That edict was good for one year as I recall. Soon thereafter the Student Council became the sponsor of the vending machines. Those machines became what casinos are today for the Native Americans: SUPER INCOME!!! The Student Council was quickly buying a new football scoreboard, repaving the track; it even agreed to finance the set-building for plays. The Student Council now regularly had a healthy account of $10,000 or so; the Student Council for the first time ever–COUNTED!

Occasionally, the Lobby–the maintenance of it– became a major problem: there were numerous wastebaskets, all properly marked for the correct recycle contents and neatly provided with a plastic liner. But slobby students (a minority to be sure) would toss the half-eaten contents of one or another of the fifty choices, and slop the diet coke all over the Lobby floor. Once in a great while the VENDING MACHINES WERE SHUT DOWN FOR AN ENTIRE DAY. Surely at a loss of many hundreds of dollars to the Student Council.

Apparently, however, the CEO's of the Student Council had their own methods for enforcing the wastebasket rules: eventually just the THREAT of a shut down was good enough, and a relative truce was effected between the Slobs and the Tidies.

There was a Teachers' Dining Room just off the Cafeteria. For years one of its plain four walls was graced with an oil painting, about ten by four feet, of three workmen laying ties for a railroad. There were various rumors about the painting—it had been an award-winner in a contest the year the school was built; it had been donated to the school by the family of a graduate who had been tragically killed; it had just been left. The workmen looked rather Polish American; all of them looked alike and looked a lot like one of my brothers-in-law. Fact was: it HAD been some student's award and HAD been left in the dining room years ago. About five years ago the dining room was repainted in time for a Mid-Atlantic States Evaluation. The oil painting was never put back. This was the time also when the top of the spare refrigerator in one corner of the dining room was cleaned of miscellaneous debris; the INSIDE of the refrigerator was cleaned, too (sometimes teachers left goodies in this extra refrigerator and forgot they had left them). And the air conditioner was fixed; the tables in the room were given blue plastic covers, compliments of the Principal's wife–she also added small pots of white plastic flowers.

Once, at a neighboring high school I had noted the very effective murals of local historic places, created by talented art students of the school. Back at Bexley, I suggested we might do likewise. Dr. Lewis, head of the Latin Department, felt he might do something about this Project. Alas, before he could initiate the plan, he transferred to his wife's hometown. I did not find contagious enthusiasm in the Art Department.

In all 26–years that I taught at Bexley, there was never a trace of that department's expertise donated to the school. Individual students won many prestigious awards–Scholastic Gold Keys–their portfolios went on to be judged in New York. Amazingly fine water colors, oils, charcoal drawings, as well as clay pots, sculpted figures–all would be on display from time to time, but NOT ONE SINGLE PIECE, or a copy of any piece, ever remained to grace the long, sterile hallways. Except, that strange railroad oil painting, for years in the Teachers' Dining Room.

Several of the "old timer teachers" took trays to the Lounge, instead of eating in the Dining Room. It was possible to go out to lunch legally, but with the 27 minute time allotted, one could go out only if one lived just five minutes away as I did. In which case one would have time to microwave the hot dog in one's own microwave. I did this only if I had forgotten something at home, or if I had to make a very important phone call.

One of the real benefits of being on a fieldtrip or contest excursion was EATING OUT. Eating a fine lunch, like a civilized person. Chewing carefully. Using a real napkin. Having a cloth table cover. After I returned from one such event, my substitute had left the following note for me: "Something hysterical just happened. I feel like Lucille Ball! I went to lunch in the Cafeteria and bought a salad. When I was done the Cafeteria was empty (Thank God!) Because of this, however, I had no crowd to follow in disposing of my garbage, so I looked for the usual trashcans by the square hole in the wall. Failing to see this, I asked a cafe worker who directed me with a wave of her hand to a conveyor system hidden in the corner. I had never seen anything quite like it. Should I place the full tray on it? Should I sit down on it, holding my trash-laden tray? Should I dump the food and utensils on it? Whatever shall I do?? Impulsively I set my whole tray on it. Soon the quiet was broken by a cacophony of crunching and grinding. I had sent a large fiberglass tray to a cruel end in the jaws of a gigantic garbage disposal. The cafeteria workers came running in horror and disbelief. The worst of it was that I became incapacitated with laughter. Even now I can hardly hold in my giggles..."

With the coming of ecological awareness, the gigantic garbage disposal was shut down forever. Nowadays, three robust cafeteria workers are in the square hole behind large pans of ammonia sudsy; they await the washable soup bowls and the stainless steel forks and spoons. There are wastebaskets for small cardboard biodegradable plates, paper napkins and waxed paper from the pizza. The trays are stacked, somewhat haphazardly, by the students. No plastic, no Styrofoam—all cans and bottles in the proper recycle bin.

"Under Cherry-trees soup,
the salad, fish and all...
seasoned with petals"

-Basho

Letters From Home

"If you were really going to teach a kid values—you know, turn him around from relying on violence to settle his problems—you'd have to do that when he's in kindergarten. To wait 'til he's a freshman in high school is crazy! He's not going to change that late..."

Several church education committee members were sitting around, mulling over possible topics for Senior Highs during the summer months ahead. The comment about teaching values was made by a teacher in the public schools. We agreed with her: by thirteen, fourteen, a teen-ager would be very hard to re-train.

We were only half-right, of course. I remembered Carlos. Carlos must have been about fourteen when I first met him in Speech class. He was very good looking—had black, curly hair, was well-dressed, likeable. On the down side: he was disrup-tive, overly talkative, and concentrating hard on flunking Speech.

I sent home a progress report to that effect; two days later I received the following handwritten letter on pale grey vellum:

Dear Mrs. Juditz,

      Carles Genzalez is eur grandsen, and my husband and I are rightfully cencerned. He is living new at eur heuse (as advised by the Children's Service) because he has temperarily wern eut his mether by his actiens ever since secend grade. She has always had him under special ceunseling threugh scheel advice. She has had ceunseling with Mr. Rentner at the Yeuth Assessment Clinic in Parksville. Whatever it is that makes Carles act as he dees, (whether Auditery Perceptien Diserder er what) he still must BEHAVE IN CLASS. If Detentien is the answer, please use it. He says he is bered in classes. We will ceeperate any way yeu suggest. (Yeu must dread having him in class). We just wanted yeu te knew we realize yeu have a preblem.

      Sincerely,
      Reselyn Baker

P.S. This special report on skateboards has been the most excitement he has shown in any class. Thanks for this assignment.

As I recall, the year with Carlos went along swervingly, rather like that skateboarding. Carlos was often in Detention (at the request of some of his other teachers); I believe he did finish the course, passingly. I lost track of him in the next couple of years, but occasionally I would notice his name on the special absentee list and surmise that he was in some kind of trouble.

Three years later, on a May evening, I was walking through the exhibits in the Living Arts Festival. This was an annual event held in the Gym, a juried show of oils, water colors, photo studies, metal sculpture, handcrafted furniture and more. In the center of the room was a special space always reserved for BEST OF SHOW. This year's piece was an exquisite coffee table of rectangular design, 18th century style, created with specially selected mahogany, enhanced by inlay veneers. There was a card explaining that this piece would be sent on for national judging in Connecticut. Beneath the shining blue ribbon was the name of the student who had created the table—Carlos Gonzales.

I stood there, staring.

And I felt so pleased to think that in spite of all the befuddled counselors, the bumbling mother and grandparents, the doles of detention and the portentous progress reports—CARLOS HAD SUCCEEDED.

How had he managed to find Woodshop? As a course filler? Because he liked the noisy sound of it, the same way he caught on to skateboarding? Because he liked the teacher? (Not all students liked that Woodshop teacher—one former student with an attitude somewhat like that of Carlos had been expelled after he bit the teacher's ear).

Before the days of Carlos there was another extra-ordinarily talented student, a superb singer, but an absolute ass in class ("ass" meaning a "stubborn, doltish, mulish" type). Constantly he was in and out of schools—our high school, private schools, military schools. The Bexley Hills Director of Vocal Music found him especially irritating and refused to give him any substantial roles in musicals. At present, that alumnus is with the Metropolitan Opera; the vocal director has been deceased these many years, so he is spared the embarrassment of knowing how wrong he was. Surely it was Carlos' good fortune to find a teacher when he needed him most. In the case of the-boy-with-superior-bass-voice there is an interesting footnote: South Shore School District recently wished to bring the opera singer to Bexley Hills as a fund raising event for the South Shore Foundation. The purpose of the Foundation is to provide certain cultural opportunities for those students who would not have such enrichment otherwise. Never allowed to sing when he was a student at Bexley, now, twenty-five years later, he is to be an alumnus-who-will-inspire-today's-students. There is an exquisite kind of irony here, somewhat difficult to sort out. Perhaps if we called in a counselor...

But more about messages from home. Not all letters appeared on pale gray vellum; not all letters were written in such a spirit of willing cooperation as that of Roselyn Baker. One autumn day I received this letter, with no margins, written in pencil on tablet paper:

Mrs. Juditz,

I would appreciate if you would
believe my daughter when she tells you
that Kathi Frank is calling her names.
She's been doing this for quite sometime.
For once Dottie got fed up with the names
she was calling her so she grabbed ahold
her and shook her. Now my husband and I do
not appreciate my daughter coming home with
her fingers and hands all cut up and her
clothes tore. Clothes are not cheap I'm
sure you know that. So if your not going
to do something about this girl calling my
daughter bad an obscene names I'm going to
do something about it myself. If I have to
call my eldest daughter, you see she knows
Mr. Wilson the principal very well, she
was his favorite student when she went to
that school. She'll go right to him. She's
the type of girl you don't feol with.

Thank you,

Mrs. Anna Kasdic, Foster Parent

There was more than one problem with this letter: I could not easily identify the daughter who had been called obscene names (no teachers have personal copies of parental names), and I had no idea who the daughter was who was not to be fooled with. I could, however, identify Kathi. Kathi was possibly the most unusual student I ever had. Technically speaking, she was identified as an aphasic child—an individual with loss or impairment of the power to use or comprehend words, usually resulting from a brain lesion. Actually, Kathi's. mother had never given permission to have Kathi tested for any problem. Mother had said, "Kathi is just the way her Dad was when he was that age. She'll outgrow it." By state law, if the parents or guardian do not give permission for testing, NO TESTING. The school nurse and guidance counselor, however, agreed that aphasia was probably Kathi's problem. Kathi never talked in any class setting. Obviously she must have talked briefly to that other student, Dottie. Other students usually taunted Kathi first, then Kathi would hit and scratch and throw sharp objects. In class she kept her eyes downcast, sometimes she glanced furtively at other students, and she frequently picked her nose. This latter habit was what usually started the taunting by other students.

There were, however, a couple of ways that Kathi participated in class. In English class she would sometimes write complete sentences. As soon as she had written these sentences she would quickly erase them, then start to write again, then erase. Her goal seemed to be a blank page by the end of the period. In Speech class, she would be willing to go to the speaker's platform for a news report. She would begin to read aloud from the paper, and she would not stop. If permitted, she would have continued reading until the end of the period and perhaps on until the end of the day.

Except on one afternoon, when we were gathered in small groups to read aloud a play, something extraordinary happened. Kathi's group was preparing to read from Ted Tally's "Terra Nova." Suddenly Kathi came to life, stopped working at her nose, and in a complete sentence asked to read the part of "Kathy". She read it, even read it with some expression, and became only mildly hostile when we reached the end of Kathy's speeches.

Those were her moments of participation. Nothing else.

All writing erased. Always silent. Whether or not she ever outgrew this behavior, I never knew. Nor did I ever learn if the "girl not to be fooled with" ever showed up at the Principal's office.

On occasion a letter from home would be an apology, as in the case of a Mom who had missed an Assembly where her son had received a First Place Award for his original radio play in state competition. She had never had a chance to hear the tape before it had been sent off for state judging; she called me to ask if she could please have the tape for a few days at home. I sent it off promptly, pleased with her interest.

Four days later, the following note was in my school mailbox:

Dear Mrs. Juditz,

Thank you f or the tape. I enjoyed
it. Unfortunately, I made the recorder's
greatest-feared-error. I inadvertently
erased the first couple minutes of the
tape, I don't know how to adequately
express myself. All I can say is, please
forgive me. I have taped many tapes and
records and have never done this before. I
don't know how I could have done this when
I was being so careful. The tape begins
with the end of the narrator's first
lines. It is a terrible loss because there
is now no orientation to the story. You
probably hesitated when I asked to do
this, but I never thought I'd be so feel-
ish or I wouldn't have requested the loan
of the tape. I truly am sorry. If there is
another copy somewhere that you'd like to
purchase, I'll be glad to pay for it. (I
doubt another copy exists). I don't know
what else to say except I'm sorry.

        Sincerely,

        Mrs. Jane Hartman

Extra scripts we had, extra tapes, no. I sent Mrs. Hartman a complimentary script, told her all was forgiven and to have a happy summer.

Once, just once, there was this unusual typed letter from a parent:

Dear Mrs. Juditz:

It gives me great pleasure to write this letter as a parent, and as an administrator in the South Shore School District. Every teacher knows that they hear from parents and administrators immediately when something goes wrong, but hardly ever hear a word about all the quality things they do for students.

When Sara entered Bexley Hills, I was concerned about my daughter entering the big, bad world of high school. Your support, encouragement and understanding made the ninth grade transition year a most enjoyable experience... You showed her that hard work and a desire for excellence would lead to a most exciting and satisfying year.

I appreciate that philosophy so much. Sara could not have had a more successful ninth grade experience. You helped lead and support her in a very caring way. You

rewarded her for good work, but always
encouraged her to work harder. Speech class
was a very valuable part of her learning
experience.

Sara could not have had a better
year in the most expensive private academy.
Thank you for helping to make that
possible. You are a fine teacher and a
great asset to our school district. You
will have my gratitude forever. Thank you!
Raymond W. Fulton

Mr. Fulton was Director of Pupil Services; I had met
him briefly at "Back to School Night". Administrators kept a
much lower profile than Board members or teachers. If a
copy of this letter had ever been entered in my dossier, I am
sure the principal who was dismissing me to meet his budget needs, would have given it scant attention. I don't know
how long Mr. Fulton served the district, but Mr. Harvey's
tenure was stretched to the breaking point in the mid-90's at
the close of the school year when there was a food fight in
the cafeteria on the last day Seniors were present. Amidst
the lusty shouting and the mess of flying pizza buns and
succotash, Mr.Harvey's feeble attempt to restore order went
unnoticed. He was last seen that afternoon, unlatching a
cafeteria window, jumping down three feet into the veg-
etable garden, a year-end project of the General Science
Department. He did not fade totally from South Shore, however: he was transferred the following season to a middle

school at the far edge of the large South Shore District.

Contrary to popular opinion, letter writing is not a lost art. And considering the shortage of phones in the average high school, the wise parent will use paper and a writing instrument to get the teacher's attention.

"Our brightest blazes of gladness
are commonly kindled
by unexpected sparks."

       -Samuel Johnson, author,
       lexicographer
       From 'Universal Chronicle'
       (London, May 26, 1759)

Weapons!

When the Columbine High School massacre occurred at Littleton, Colorado on April 20th, 1999, Bexley Hills already had a weapons policy in place, for about six years.

Before we peruse the policy I think I should point out that I believe a very unusual set of circumstances set the stage for the massacre: there were two exceedingly bright, amoral teen-agers who were exceptionally close buddies—one a leader, the other a follower. They were exceptionally good actors without trying to be. They were irrational. For months before the massacre there were clues in the writings and discussions of Eric Harris and Dylan Klebold about their violent plans; their break-in and robbery of a van brought attention from the police, resulting in probation and sessions of conflict resolution, which the police interpreted as successful.

William Ury, an anthropologist-turned-negotiator (he led the first face-to-face sessions of Russian and Chechen leaders after a cease-fire in 1997) has said "What did we learn from Columbine? That so many people in the community knew something, but did nothing." In other words, classmates, teachers, counselors, relatives—gambled. The close of school was not far off; considering the frantic activity in the last few weeks of school-testing, sports events, field trips, proms—perhaps all those people thought "we'll soon be out of here".

Now to look at Bexley's Weapons Policy.

Weapons

Item: South Shore School District Policy
218.1
Weapons Definition: Weapon. For purposes of
these rules and regulations, the term
WEAPON shall include, but not be limited to
any knife, cutting instrument, cutting tool,
num-chuck stick, firearm, bb-gun, pellet
gun, shotgun, rifle, and/or any other tool,
instrument, or implement capable of inflict-
ing serious bodily injury. Weapons shall
include look alike or replica weapons which
are not necessarily operable.

It is fairly obvious that the writer (the Second
Assistant to the Superintendent, who conducted workshops
on Thinking Skills) had let slip past him the fact that some
definitions can be so broad as to be meaningless.

According to the definition neither a student nor a
teacher, nor cook nor custodian, could ever have a scis-
sors, paring knife, cake knife, corsage pin, safety pin,
straight pin, bottle opener, nail file, compass, razor blade,
nor a pebble from a potted plant.

About the pebble. Ken was a bully—a corpulent pim-
ply bully who told me frequently, "My teacher last year was
a good teacher I got A's in English. I LIKED English, I don't
like to write. I don't like to read. I've never read a book."

Ken sat in the first seat in a middle row. I hadn't purposely assigned him this seat—it was just the way the alpha-
bet honored him. His last name started with an "H", and he

was in about the middle of things. He was vulnerable, but I didn't know that until later.

Ken often picked on other kids: little annoyances mostly, backed up by a big mouth. One day, a smooth-looking, basically nasty boy, let Kenner have it. Nasty Boy allegedly shot a pebble from the plant on the windowsill, expertly, as Ken turned round–far enough around to receive the pebble right in his eye. Ken howled, a realistic howl, not a fake howl. He was grabbing his eye. He was turning red and blubbery. Ken, for the first time in that class, was really hurt. I sent him to the lav for cooling waters. Eventually he returned, not looking much better, and he was angry. I sent him to the nurse. Finally he came back with a report that he should be checked by an eye doctor. By the end of the day I had submitted my incident report to the Principal. As it turned out, the Principal had already received and read the nurse's report and filed a report to me: How on earth could there be a rock in the plant?????? REMOVE THE PLANT IMMEDIATELY!!!! In 25 years of teaching, always with plants, I had never had a student create a lethal weapon from a potted plant. Ken did visit an eye doctor; the doctor pronounced the eye healthy. Kenner was still a loud-mouth bully, but he didn't turn around quite as often, and as far as I know, alleged Nasty Boy at the rear of the room was always just as sly, suave, and low profile all the way to his Senior year.

Were there real weapons in school? Yes. In the early 70's the son of an elementary school principal in the District, during a highly hostile mood swing, pulled from his jacket a very business-like knife, put it on his deak and muttered what I took to be a few dire threats to me. I told him to put the knife away, right away, and he did. I'm not sure what course of action I might have taken if he had decided to do otherwise.

Guns? Mostly we had them in plays each year, before state law prohibited firearms in school; I also had some very effective gun cleaning demonstrations, about one per class each autumn. The absolutely most beautiful demonstration I ever witnessed was the skinning of a rabbit which the student had shot on his way to school. This was a distinguished honor student, straight A' s. A student with an environmental awareness, a student whose educational goal was to major in science, whose career goal was forest management. As far as I know, he reached both those goals. It was not until the Spring of '93 when I was about to retire from Bexley, that we had the first major gun incident. A simple-minded student, one who always stood outside the classroom door with his nose pasted to the glass, brought a handgun to school because he thought his buddy was going to murder him. His buddy was not simple-minded. Trevor was quite smart and hostile enough to make you believe he wanted to murder many people. To me, he would often say, when asked for a pass after his late arrival for an 8 am class, "Shut up you fuckin' bitch!" Then he would storm from the room, slamming the door; he never managed to break the glass, but the flag affixed to the upper ledge of the bulletin board always flipped to upside down. The incident of the two Freshmen boys and the illegal firearm marked the start of trouble, with weapons and the writing of Weapons Policy #218.1. Rather like the policy on Obscene Language, the definition was so broad as to be almost unenforceable.

Farther along in the edict on weapons is this injuncture: "Staff members are to keep supervised school activities or course requirements involving the possession of weapons to a minimum. To that end, staff members are encouraged to find alternate means of conducting activities or courses where weapons might be brought to school or school sponsored activities.

For example, rather than allowing props to be brought for a speech assignment, "have the student bring a picture of the item."

Well now. No more earthworm dissection? No frog cutting apart? Nor cat skinning? No exacto knife work in art class? (Only BAKED potatoes in Home Ec? No metal shop nor wood shop? Remember the incident of that unstable student who bit the wood shop teacher's ear? They were natural teeth, difficult to leave at home.

My point is: weapons are everywhere. The real weapons—guns, switch-blades, num chucks—are properly outlawed in these bad times. In better times, these weapons were often there, but we didn't feel threatened.

The pebble in the plant is not the problem: the problem is the student who threw the pebble—his insensitivity, his amoral reaction to his peers; worse, his inability to empathize with another human being. In fourteen short years, why did he turn out like this?

He's clean-cut, good-looking even, well-spoken.

Unlike Trevor, who threatened the simple-minded buddy. Trevor is always angry in daily interaction with peers, teachers and his grandma with whom he lives. Harmony Wells, who lives near Trevor, mentioned to me that Trevor's grandma always buys him something very nice when he gets into trouble at school. His latest gift was a new TV for his room.

Nasty Boy is unlike Ken, the bully. Ken is a whiner, is an obvious trouble-maker; Nasty Boy is polite, feigns enthusiasm, he might win many votes in a school election.

A recent study by the Gun Safety Institute in Cleveland's third through 12th graders has shown that many children don't understand the difference between being assertive in life and being aggressive toward people. The study identified four Attitudes that make young people want to turn to gun use: guns, and the people who use them, are exciting; guns provide safety and power; physical aggression is acceptable behavior; if offended or shamed, one's pride can be restored only by violent aggression. This information was included in an article by David Holmstrom, "Out of Harm's Way, Protecting Children from Violence", printed in the Christian Science Monitor (Sept 1996).

At the close of the 1998 school year the Center on Juvenile and Criminal Justice, Washington, D.C., published its report on child deaths in America. There had been 40 people, including adults, who were shot and killed at school during 1997-98; eleven children were killed in the five highly publicized incidents—Pearl, Mississippi; West Paducah, Kentucky; Jonesboro, Arkansas; Edinboro, Pennsylvania and Springfield, Oregon.

Eleven is also the number of children who die in two days due to family violence (meaning child abuse or neglect) by parents or guardians. Eight is the number of children killed by gunfire every day. 3,024 is the number of children killed by gunfire every year, the vast majority at the hands of adults. According to these recent statistics, school still IS A SAFE PLACE.

How has Bexley Hills High School reacted to the reality of violence? In-school drug tests have been considered. In 1998 the concept was both praised and criticized at a school board study session. No decision was reached. What else has South Shore District done? Teachers were given violence training and taught the importance of being calm amid chaos.

Both these actions remind us that when tragedies occur, targets for blame are usually drugs, unobservant teachers, along with abusive parents, easy access to guns, too much TV watching and sensational news media reports. When drugs are mentioned, technically that includes booze, but the people outside of school always think pot, cocaine, heroin or LSD. With Bexley students, it's the booze that counts.

About the necessity for staff to remain calm amid chaos: many years ago the Bexley teachers' "cool in crisis" was well tested by the frequent bomb scares of the 60's and early 70's, and by the accident at Three Mile Island. We had 1800 students in those days, in a school built for 1400 students. I don't remember any teacher ever panicking. One math teacher did leave at the time of the accident at TMI—his wife arrived to pick him up at noon that day. After another couple of seasons, he left Bexley permanently to become a state politician, but that's an entirely different story.

How to start to turn a student around, whether he be Ken the Bully, Trevor the Hostile, or Nasty Boy with the pebble?

Since the mid-seventies, psychiatrists working with teenagers say it's a waste of time and effort to look for places to put the blame. Yes, short-term solutions would include locking up the guns and the alcohol, but the long-term solution lies in conflict resolution, which surely should begin with the pre- schooler, but can also be taught to older students with success.

"Conflict resolution" is not "therapy"—it is the teaching of social skills. If there have been units of conflict resolution introduced into the curriculum at Bexley, there has been no reporting of this strategy in district newsletters nor in local newspapers. Nor has there been any mention as to whether or not any students from South Shore District attended the '98 summer seminar for benefits from training on non-violence organized by the regional Girl Scout Council. If anyone from South Shore had attended, he/she would have learned the principles of non-violence followed by Mahatma Gandhi and Dr. Martin Luther King, Jr.

SIX Principles ef NONvielence (King)

Nenvielence
1.is a way ef life fer ceurageeus peeple
2.seeks te win friendship and understanding
3.seeks te defeat injustice, net peeple
4.helds that suffering can educate and
transferm
5.cheeses leve instead ef hate
6.believes that the universe is en the
side ef justice

The summer seminar, I understand, lasted for two days.

The 40 to 50 teen-agers attending learned words such as "agape" which means unconditional love for all (including adversaries), and the word "ahisma", a Sanskrit word for noninjury, made popular by Gandhi. Civil disobedience, conscientious objection, boycotts and other organized, nonviolent resistance strategies were subjects explored to help students reach their goals through peaceful means.

Surely it is impossible to gauge the degree of positive long-term benefit from the program, but at least this seems to be the right starting track.

Thomas D. Zweifel, CEO of the Swiss Consulting Group in New York, is a coach and lecturer on leadership. In an essay (The Christian Science Monitor 9/22/98) Mr. Zweifel stated: "If listening were a standard discipline taught and tested in schools ... major social issues and costs might be avoided...in politics, diplomacy, negotiation and personal relationships. In other words, amazing things can happen if we are still and listen for a change."

In my own curriculum for the 9th grade speech course at Bexley, I had included a special unit on Listening, not the listening for the usual Speaker-Audience situation. This was listening on a one-to-one basis, a situation where someone comes to you with a P R O B L E M...

First of all, I would caution the class, there are two things you may not do: you cannot just turn away from this person, pretending you didn't hear what he or she was trying to tell you. In the second place, you cannot change the subject.

Now then—here's what you "do" if you want to be a really good listener for this person with the problem:

1. Avoid giving any advice
2. Avoid asking questions
3. Avoid sympathizing
4. Avoid analyzing the situation

All of the above are the strategy most of us want to use, especially giving advice.

I would continue the lesson by giving a rather ordinary "problem" example: Suppose that a friend who rides with you every day on the bus says to you tomorrow morning, "I'm telling you, I'm really worried. I'm going to flunk

Algebra this semester... there's just no way I can get a passing grade."

You, if you're the advice-giving listener, will say "Mary Jo, what you need to do is find yourself a tutor, maybe for the next four weeks."

If you're the listener who asks questions, you'll be firing at Mary Jo, "Who's your teacher? Do you have homework every night? What were your grades on the last two big tests?"

Or, if you're feeling very sorry for Mary Jo by this time, you'll commiserate with, "Now Mary Jo, honestly, you'll get through this. Even in the worst-case scenario, remember how good your grades are in history and English... Well, you can make up this math stuff in Summer School."

Finally, if you're going to search deeply to discover why Mary Jo dug herself into this pit in the first place, you'll tell her, "You know what the problem really is, Mary Jo? Your Algebra teacher missed a lot of school in the first two months of the year. All those substitutes really got you confused..."

By this point most students cannot imagine what else to do as a listener, but there actually is a Number Five in the listening process: paraphrase. To be sure, there are some 9th graders who are-unfamiliar with this word. I explain–to paraphrase is simply to say briefly, in your own words, what Mary Jo has been saying. "Mary Jo, you're telling me that "you believe you're going to have a lot of trouble passing Algebra..."

And then, Mary Jo, being human, will begin telling

you a great deal more than you want to know about her dilemma in Algebra I, but you can be assured that she will be grateful to you forever for having been such a good listener.

Recently I was talking with a former teacher and mentioned "conflict resolution" and the need to include it in the school curriculum.

"I never heard of it," she said. "How on earth would you put together a course on that????"

"Well," I said, "you could begin with a unit on listening. Reinforcement for the listening skills that might or might not have been absorbed in Speech class."

She rather skillfully managed to change the subject. But as I thought more about the possibility for such a course, I figured that perhaps unit two could focus on manners, which again is practicing good communication skills. Probably unit three would be the toughest to teach: how to cooperate instead of compete. From Day One at Kindergarten to Graduation evening thirteen years later, "competition" is the word carved in concrete.

Nadine Epstein, writer, artist and mother in Washington. D.C., explained in a recent opinion essay in the Monitor (1/5/99),"Every child, parent and teacher should learn conflict resolution skills—how to talk out a problem, compromise, negotiate, search out creative options, channel anger, avoid violence, empathize, tolerate, understand, and how to listen and be aware of their feelings.... If we have learned anything from the current culture war, it is that America, the world's supreme economic and military power, has much in common with a dysfunctional family. We need to arm all of our children with wisdom appropriate for our times.

The Weapons Code of South Shore District, for all its inclusiveness, made no mention of a small object I had kept at the back of my classroom desk drawer, buried under office forms and attendance records. I had never intended this object as a weapon. I had found it one day at the bottom of a storage carton, decided it might be useful somehow and tossed it in with some hardware miscellany at the back of the desk drawer. The object was a small rectangle of wood, about 3x5, and 1-inches thick. Protruding from the wood were four steel pins, each one inch in length.

On a March afternoon (it must have been March—the longest, grimmest month of the school year)—I was teaching a class in broadcasting; there were twelve students. We had been listening to a recording by Edward R. Murrow, one of his broadcasts from the rooftops of London during WWII. We had had some discussion about the tape, I then reviewed the assignment for the next session and asked for two volunteers to help bring a couple of props baskets from the stage area. Two boys volunteered. This was a class I could trust to wait until the bell rang, if I were gone for a few minutes. The trip to the stage area was short...I could go with the volunteers, return by the time the bell was ringing—the boys would not be late for the next class.

That's how the scene played out: we were returning from the stage as the bell was ringing; the boys set the baskets of props inside the room as other students were leaving, then picked up their backpacks and left, too.

Four minutes later, at the start of the next class, I went to the desk for the seating chart and attendance forms. My chair was in its usual place, but on it was the rectangle with the steel pins. In the deep desk drawer everything looked normal–the attendance forms, with the other office forms beneath the same box of hardware items. Perhaps inherent in the teacher's classroom code is the directive: Look around carefully before you sit down. Even in the class you trust, there is someone with anger and frustration thinly disguised.

"Our brightest blazes of gladness are commonly kindled by unexpected sparks."

-Samuel Johnson, author, lexicographer
From 'Universal Chronicle'
(London, May 26, 1759)

A Level Three Offense

"I suppose you realize this will have to go into your file..."

Mr. Hoover, the assistant principal, continued to shuffle papers, I surmised this was the paper work for my "case". In another few moments I would begin to feel that I had committed the theft of my keys and thrown them down an upstairs toilet. In the span of twenty-six and a half years of teaching at Bexley Hills High School, I had had to report a number of thefts: I was always encouraged to feel guilty.

The first theft I did NOT report to the Principal. I reported the theft to the boy's mother, who thanked me for reporting, but the stopwatch that had been stolen did not reappear. Larry was a boy big for his age, who always had a knowing smirk on his face. He seemed too old to steal a stopwatch just for the moment's thrill. It took me another several months to discover that boys only stole stopwatch-es: they stole them to time their cars. How many watches were stolen through the years? One, sometimes two, dis-appeared in. a year–altogether count 40 or 50. 1 started my teaching career using reliable thirty-dollar watches; I ended my career using Made-in-Taiwan watches at $9.99 each. On one occasion a speech contest judge, an adult, bor-rowed my watch on competition day. It was not returned. Perhaps he didn't think 9.99 was worth the phone call or the trip over to my home.

Of the felonious crimes committed in high schools, theft outstrips all others. In 1996, thefts accounted for 62 percent of all crime against students, with 79 thefts for every 1,000 students aged 12 to 18; on the average there were 46 thefts for every 1,000 teachers from 1993 to 1996.

Theft is every day. Students steal from other students. Students steal from teachers. Unidentified beings steal after school hours. Visiting students steal–visiting to participate in sports events, plays, concerts, conferences. What is stolen, aside from stopwatches? Obviously, all kinds of other equipm.ent. We once had a run on weights and measures from the science labs to aid in drug sales. Tools, ladders (even one I had chained to the backstage wall), the book of Drama Club Minutes, small glass birds, tickets!–the teacher in the Graphics Department had trouble printing play tickets because the printers pocketed the tickets. Electronics equipment, of course. Bird prints–maybe by the same person who stole the glass birds?

And grade books. At the close of an early Spring day, in a very large, bad class, my grade book, always in the middle of my desk (school rule decreed it be there), was MISSING. The students were already filing from the room; I checked the waste basket–no grade book. A girl near the end of the line-up turned to whisper to me, "I know who took it". She gave me the name.

I rushed through the line. The boy named was already headed for the buses, invisible in the crush of other students. There were five, no SIX smelly-buses lined up along the porch outside the hallway. I sprinted onto the first bus. No Ray. Second, still no Ray. Third bus, fourth bus–in the back, hands in jacket pocket, jacket looking very bulging. I swooped down on Ray. Actually, Ray was pretty small to begin with, and standing there, glaring at him, I had a certain brief advantage. "I want my grade book. GIVE IT

TO ME!" I said, my voice projecting clearly over the engine noise and the babble of 39 other students.

Ray handed over the book; it was doubled up, the wire spine bent. But it was intact. Up to that day, I had had some misgiving about the idea of students informing on other students. As the seasons went by, more and more we had to rely on the narkers to find the troublemakers.

What else was stolen? Candy. Great boxes of candy that had been ordered to use as a fundraiser, stolen by somebody in the club that was doing the fund raising. Master keys, closet keys. The purpose of these thefts was not to use the keys directly, but to make other keys and sell the keys at $5.00 each. What else? A smoking jacket from a play costume rack, allegedly by the play's lead actor. Theatre books, including "The Effect of Gamma Rays on Man-in-the-Moon Marigolds." From the props room housing the set dressing for "George M", a potted palm, value $100.00. A piece of fake Egyptian papyrus from the back wall of my classroom, value $10.00.

And my corsage for graduation. At that point in time we had a principal who believed that all female faculty members involved in the ceremony should wear an orchid. These were paid for from the principal's special fund, duly ordered and stored for the day in the refrigerator in the Teachers' Dining Room, to be picked up on graduation evening by the so-named teachers. Some quirk of fate led me to the refrigerator early in the afternoon at the end of classes. The box with my name was there, I opened it: NO CORSAGE on the little nest of white shredded paper. There was still time to go to the florist, buy my own replacement corsage and be back for the ceremonies at 6 pm. It was for moments like this that I had always lived within five minutes driving time of the school. The florist had no more white orchids, but he did have a pale, pale green. I took it.

Sometimes the speed and logistical expertise with which a theft occurs is amazing. One afternoon I was moving props into the stage area when a rather battered leatherette chair broke down outside the stage door. A leg had come undone. I propped open the stage door, went back-stage to get a hammer and a few nails. I heard the 5-minute bell ring, I flicked on a few more lights and went back to work on my chair. IT WAS GONE. NEVER TO BE SEEN AGAIN.

Money??? Every day at least one person's locker was broken into. Almost every day somebody's pocket was picked. This was routine. But for me, on occasion, there were interesting twists. Twin students apparently rifled my handbag one November afternoon and gleaned $88.00 (meant mostly for the turkey shopping). In those days, no locks on Teacher's desk; and no room cabinet with a lock. A handbag stayed at the teacher's desk; usually the desk was an off-limits place to students. But the twins were in front of the room doing some tape recording at the speaker's table, while I was reviewing material with another student. Apparently one twin took a side trip to the desk.

And, next to the last day of another-school year, in the era when pocket books were often baskets-with-decorative-covers, I happened to have a small class of seven students: the other class members had been Seniors and were already gone from school. At the end of the class session that afternoon I noticed that my wallet was not beneath the cover of the handbag. Well, not to worry too much. Such a small class. I took the list of names to the office where I expected all seven to be called down at once to the nurse and principal for personal search. I had not reckoned with the bomb scare already in progress. No time to search MY seven–all administrators were searching for the bomb, along with the police squad.

I had never had a wallet stolen before!!! I could live without stopwatches, glass birds, eighty-eight dollars, my graduation corsage, but an ENTIRE WALLET...with cards, pictures, addresses, lists.... MY WORLD!?! The day ended. Five of the seven students were finally searched, no wallet was found of course. That evening I had an anonymous phone call; I thought I recognized a voice from the class." Did you lose your wallet today?" the caller inquired. Before I could answer, there was a muffled giggle, the caller hung up. I continued to call credit card companies and local stores. At about 8 pm the doorbell rang. A pleasant looking gentleman, a neighbor from two blocks over, handed me my wallet. It had been tossed into his trashcan. The $3.60 was missing but all else was intact. It was at least two years before all the credit card confusion was sorted out.

What is NOT stolen? Clothes. Which I'm sure will surprise readers because many school districts in the past few years have been considering mandatory uniforms "to prevent clothes theft and improve discipline". So be it, but when I left Bexley in '93, very few students' clothes were ever stolen. Great quantities of clothes were left behind each year, so great that several days were devoted to putting these piles of clothes on display tables at the end of the year (to give losers a chance to be finders); what remained was hauled off to Goodwill. True, Bexley was a school with a large socio-economic middle class, but at least ten percent were from families near poverty level.

But back to what I really wanted to tell you about the "non-stealing" of clothes. I once left a very handsome nutria fur coat back stage on an unseasonably warm winter's day.

Play directors have days where things are so confused and out of shape, there's nothing else to do but go home late and start out early the next day. I didn't even remember my coat until three days later! It was still at the same place, unharmed. There had been rehearsals, study halls in the auditorium, with many students passing back stage. A leath-erette chair, a potted palm, wouldn't have lasted five minutes.

How to prevent theft? One started the school year wearing a suit with pockets for A) the keys for school, and B) a pen. Keys-for-school-and-a-pen must always be with Teacher. Preferably concealed in pockets. But as the year progressed, one occasionally wanted to wear a dress with no pockets, or a skirt and a woolly sweater (it was 60 degrees down there some days in Bexley North); thus, keys and pen were sometimes visible. Sometimes the keys were laid down in order to handle the recording equipment or clean up the speaker's table where a ferret, the subject of a demonstration speech, had somewhat disgraced himself. Often the pen had to be put down. I figured I had the most valuable pen ever; the pen cost 3.95 or 4.95 at the local bookshop, but it was replaced about every six weeks, 36 weeks of the year, for 26-years.

Other methods of theft prevention were tried at times. One mid-autumn morning, near the close of the first period, all staff members received this confidential memo along with the day's attendance sheet.

Printed beneath the small picture of a very pleasant looking girl was the message: "This young lady is Carolyn Devlin. Her parents wish to have all teachers know that Carolyn has a history of stealing and is under counseling professionally in order to help her overcome this problem. Please exercise due caution with Carolyn as she had already admitted two thefts this year. Fortunately Carolyn responds positively when she knows she is being watched. The family believes we can help Carolyn by removing any source of temptation and by reporting immediately any suspicious behavior. Carolyn's scheduled teachers should monitor her closely. Teachers on Hall Duty and Cafeteria Duty should be alert to her presence and would do well to recognize her on sight. Club Advisors and Coaches need to remember this information should Carolyn elect to join extra-curricular activities. Report concerns or suspicions to Miss Dillman or Mr. Farnsworth."

It was weekly procedure in mid-autumn to collect "Budget Money" from the f irst period class. On that particular morning I had collected the money, duly noted on the budget cards who had paid what, stuffed all the cash, checks and records into the Central Treasury Budget Envelope, sealed the envelope, and as was also according to rule, asked for a willing volunteer to walk the envelope to Central Treasury on Floor Two. An eager hand shot up, belonging to the pleasant, smiling face of, YOU GUESSED IT!!! Carolyn Devlin. The Confidential Memo concerning Carolyn had reached me about twenty minutes too late. I became her Third Theft of the Year.

There was at least one significant editorial (a full two column complete page "significant") at the close of a recent school year. This appeared in "The Bexley Outlook", the student newspaper. Principal Harvey was quoted as saying, "Stealing's always wrong. We do have a problem with it. Stealing is not only a school offense, it's a criminal offense". And the writer went on to say that the school has a stiff penalty for stealing. Students caught stealing face immediate suspension. Theft is a level three offense. It includes one to three days of In-School-Suspension, restitution, and criminal prosecution. No mention in this editorial that school thieves are almost never caught, that Confidential Memos about thieves arrive too late, and that in at least one other incident all of my students, for an entire day, were unwittingly placed on the Honor System.

On that day I was scheduled to escort a small cast of students to the State Theatre at New Hope—a full day's field trip. Somehow the Administration Office never finished the paper work on this particular field trip: no substitute was ever assigned. I was gone the full day with classes left totally unattended. What was stolen? A wooden Polish box from my desk, and, in the case of one class, numbers were altered in the grade book. (I learned about the grades from a narker.) The box probably graces the basement bar of some student from the class of `84.

Probably the most bizarre case of theft I encountered did not happen on school property.

On a fine winter's day I had taken our Repertory Theatre players to the newest, largest, most prestigious nursing home in the city. The play was the "Happy Journey to Camden and Trenton", by Thornton Wilder. We arrived on schedule at the home, and the friendly receptionist showed us where we would perform in the Day Lounge. Further, she showed us the two lavatories which were directly in back of her small reception room/office. Our three boys disappeared into the Men's Room, and I followed along with the girls to the Ladies' for changing and make-up.

In about ten minutes everyone was in costume; a few more minutes were devoted to moderate make-up; there were no real stage lights; one of the girls asked, "What shall we do with our clothes and things, Mrs. J?"

"Oh, I think if you just pile them up neatly right here in the corner, everything will be fine", replied the unstreetwise Mrs. J.

It was now curtain time. I introduced the play, the students performed it. There was applause from those home residents, who were still lively enough to know they were watching a play.

And we trotted back to the lavatory. In the twenty-five minutes we had been gone, the entire pile of clothing had disappeared, except for a pair of purple shoes, size four.

As I waited at the receptionist's desk (about eight feet away from the lavatory door), a call was put through to the police, who were an hour and 45 minutes in arriving. Once they showed up, I soon discovered the police were not there to investigate our theft of clothes and handbags: they were there to investigate the theft of a guest's purse and jewelry, which had occurred earlier in the day.

That "Happy Journey" finally did end. I was able to get all the theft reports filed and the students to their homes. Later in the week I was to learn who was the chief administrator of the nursing home: said gentleman had been fired about four years previously from his administrative post at the County Home because he had intercepted and sold the steaks that were being delivered for the residents' dinner.

We never recovered anything from that unfortunate field trip. Oddly enough, the incident did not go into my file. It was the only time I was NOT made to feel guilty. Actually, I did feel somewhat guilty. When I accompanied Children's Theatre casts to elementary schools, I always made sure that belongings were stowed back stage where I could keep a steely eye on things. And how could I have forgotten that when my mother was in a nursing home I had a steady problem with petty theft? I suppose I had thought the receptionist's own rest room would be safe enough. Very easily I could have plunked everything on a chair right beside me in that Day Lounge...

The writer in the "Bexley Outlook" who was explaining Principal Harvey's opinions about "a third-level offense" had concluded his editorial with, "Ironically, in an era not ready to adopt Outcome Based Education, there is a definite need to instill values and reinforce what is right and what is wrong. All of society can agree that stealing is wrong, yet not all of society is prepared to take the steps to prevent this injustice".

Some readers will remember that Outcome Based Education (OBE) meant that the student should attain a certain level of proficiency before going on to the next level of work, and "values" should be part of the learning process: respect for self and others, respect for property, understanding what is right and wrong in making a judgment.

Alas, the Christian Far Right rose up to protest. From Marilyn Quayle, all the way down to the little mothers of pre-schoolers, OBE was derided and demonized.

Which certainly surprised teachers of most subjects, who for years thought that's what they had been doing all along—teaching step by step and hoping the students would also turn out to be decent citizens.

"What you do not wish done
to yourself, do not do to others".

-Confucius

Those Who Fear Books

I have just finished reading a press release by Carole Feldman: "Teachers Do Feel Intimidation", subtitled "Fear of the Right Has Chilling Effect in Classroom".

According to the article, a teacher from Sinking Springs, PA said teachers have had problems when raising the concept of multicultural diversity. Well! For years I had been clipping coupons for the water and sewage municipal bond issue of 1964 of Sinking Springs. With such an intriguing name, I always wondered what kind of place it might be. A teacher at this school, according to the news article, had wanted to show the film, "The Last of the Mohicans". The principal said not to, and the Union said in effect–play it cool and don't show it.

By October of 1995, our state had attained the rank of third among the 50 states in school censorship. This designation was the result of a study by the People of the American Way. The report found more than censorship as a threat to students' right to learn. "This year we documented a resurgence in attempts to teach creationism, a rise in the number of efforts to push vouchers and so-called parental rights' legislation, and an alarming jump in the number of objections to materials that mention homosexuality", reported PFAW.

At Bexley Hills, the first story that ran into trouble was "A Patch of Blue", and this was in the late 60's. A white parent objected to having her daughter read this work. There was a hearing held at the district level with several English teachers, the Principal Mr. Anderson and the parent present. It was learned that the parent had never read

"Patch of Blue" she objected to the cover of the book—a simple line drawing illustration of a black man and a white girl.

"A Patch of Blue" was NOT banned from the English curriculum.

In Speech class all topics were allowed, although only one to a speaker. For example, one student in a persuasive speech series would speak FOR abortion, one could speak AGAINST.

One could speak FOR euthanasia, one AGAINST. (Most class members were surprised to learn the subject was not "Youth in Asia"). Incidentally in twenty-six years, two subjects were always used: "Capital Punishment" and Legalization of Marijuana".

When it came time to model graduation speeches, however, I banned one topic as inappropriate for the event: "Condoms Should Be Available in High School". I was not opposed to this directive, but I could not justify it for a formal graduation ceremony.

The "Right" that columnist Carole Feldman was referring to in her article, are informally called the "Fundies", the students who are fundamentalist Christians; often they keep a relatively low profile in class. There have been exceptions. One boy in a Track Two English class included some religious doctrine in every piece of his writing: "It is too bad only 4,000 persons will go to Heaven. All the rest will go to Hell." Jerome always expressed sorrow for the rest of us. As far as I could ascertain, in his English class he was the only one going to Heaven. Somewhat later that same semester however, he wrote that he was "looking for a good Christian girl who shared these same beliefs." (I did not notice any girls showing an interest).

Jerome was always so neatly dressed: carefully pressed slacks, spotless white shirt, nattily patterned neck-tie, shoes, REAL shoes, not sneakers nor docksiders–REAL SHOES, carefully shined. In fact, all of the "Fundies" looked great in the eyes of the teachers. They looked so RIGHT (no pun intended). I should say, they looked PREPPY–an entire roomful of them would have been a joy to behold, visually. But when the debate began, there actually was no debate. Their ideas, their opinions were not open for question. The most hide abound Catholics from my relatives of the 40's and 50's would have seemed extant liberals compared to these students. We were all going to Hell in a hand bas-ket–gays, blacks, the homeless, the pro-choice into the bas-ket first.

Although they often kept a low profile, some could strike back with amazing speed. Here is one incident, exactly as it happened.

It was Final Exam time. In Speech class, the exam was a Final Speech, on any topic the student had not per-sonally previously used in his/her class. A very attractive girl, Janet, gave a persuasive speech with pro-life thesis. She was appropriately dressed, used the right amount of note cards. Her delivery was excellent; she was quite sin-cere in her point of view. Her content was well organized. But, she made some totally inaccurate comments about the safety of abortion in a modern hospital. I gave her a 92 on the speech, handed her evaluation sheet to her at 11:15

am. A "92" was a B+. It had certainly sounded like an A speech, but with inaccurate content it had to be a B. Thirty minutes later, at 11:45, I received a call to report to the Assistant Principal's office. Mr. Hoover said, "Janet's father has just called me and wondered if you gave Janet a 92 on her Final because you are personally Pro-Choice?"

Without commenting on whether or not I was Pro-Choice, I explained, "Janet's speech had inaccurate information. I am the daughter of a doctor and the niece of a doctor—Janet's medical information could not be given an A rating."

Mr. Hoover made no further comment; I left the room. Janet never really spoke directly to me again. She was in Drama Club and would come to meetings where I was present. But the summer right after she graduated she waited on me in a store where she was working. She never said, "Hello, Mrs. Juditz", as did all other students who checked out my merchandise at various and sundry stores. Janet was as attractive and carefully dressed as ever; she never acknowledged that she knew me. And I thought, for sure I don't ever want Janet for my school board director.

Were books banned from the Bexley Hills Library? It was hard to tell. Some of our most conscientious librarians had left Bexley about the time the new library was built onto the school—1975. There followed for a time a succession of short-term librarians: the first one soon went into the whole-sale fine-linen business, another left when her husband was transferred to Philadelphia. Her successor neglected to order the Reader's Guide for an entire semester. My

Extemp contest speakers, therefore, had to go to a local Middle School to find their magazine materials.

Eventually, I began to notice that many cut-off dates in the card catalogue were 1974, 75, 76. The printed sheets which each teacher had routinely received, listing all the new acquisitions, seemed to have disappeared.

It was about five years into my research for this book that I really learned the answer to these problems about the Bexley Library. In 1974, the Nixon administration moved to offer federal dollars to schools in block grants. From the 1960's to '74 school libraries received rather generous specific streams of funds. But when states were given freedom to spend the money as they chose, few chose to help the libraries. And even now, a quarter of a century later, funding for school libraries has not come even close to keeping pace with growing expenses. For example, while the average cost of today's youth book is about $18.00, Philadelphia schools are allotted only $5.00 per student for new book purchases.

Perhaps the saddest note of all at Bexley: The Christian Science Monitor (our Debaters' newspaper source for reliable and non-biased material) was replaced by USA TODAY.

What has been marked for banning in our public schools throughout the country? As reported in the Newsletter on Intellectual Freedom of March 1996 through 1997, here is a sampling and the reasons for the challenge.

"I Know Why the Caged Bird Sings"
by Maya Angelou
(Too sexually explicit; doesn't represent
traditional values)

"The Scarlet Letter" by Nathaniel Hawthorne
 (Conflicts with values of the community)

"A Separate Peace" by John Knowles
(Graphic Language)

"To Kill a Mocking Bird" by Lee Harper
(Conflicts with values of the community)

"A Wrinkle in Time" by Madeleine L'Engle
(Undermines religious beliefs)

"Moby Dick" by Herman Melville
(Conflicts with values of the community)

"Beloved" by Toni Morrison
(Too violent)

"Catcher in the Rye" by J.D. Salinger
(Use of profanity)

"Twelfth Night" by William Shakespeare
(Encourages homosexuality)

"A Light in the Attic" by Shel Silverstein
(Too dreary and negative)

"Of Mice and Men" by John Steinbeck
(Use of profanity)

"The Joy Luck Club" by Amy Tan
(Conflicts with values of the community)

"The Adventures of Huckleberry Finn"
by Mark Twain
(Racially Offensive)

"Little House in the Big Weeds" by Laura
Ingalls Wilder
(Racially offensive)

"Native Son" by Richard Wright
(Sexually graphic and violent)

     This sampling did not include South Shore's very own special challenge of two or so years earlier: a parent requested that the Bible be removed from all school libraries in the district because "the book contains language and stories that are inappropriate for children of any age", including tales of incest and murder. Fortunately, the challenge was met by one of the most conservative of all South Shore board members—the Bibles stayed on the shelves of the libraries, because this board member said, "we'd be the laughing stock of the whole community if we did such a stupid thing". True, his motive was skewed, but the books stayed on.

As I mentioned at the beginning of this chapter, the banning of books by the Christian Right is not the total censorship picture. The long debated issue of evolution vs. creationism resurfaces fairly frequently; the effort to establish a voucher system of school choice (strongly endorsed by the current governor of the state), which would siphon monies away from public to parochial schools; the attempted defeat of OBE, Outcome Based Education, a program of education reform—all of these issues are a part of the censorship effort. Independent gubernatorial candidate Peg Luksik managed the fight against education reforms in Pennsylvania; eventually the reforms were approved by the State Board of Education.

People for the American Way, the liberal citizens lobbying group based in Washington D.C., also chronicles efforts by parents to have materials they consider objectionable removed from the nation's classrooms and libraries. The report also lists attempts to reintroduce voluntary school prayer. The number of books, magazines and other classroom materials challenged nationwide increased dramatically in the mid-90's; on average four in 10 challenges were successful.

The early-on librarians at Bexley had sometimes put plain covers on magazines they considered too revealing, but the magazines were there, with no passages cut, with an updated Reader's Guide, and any book a teacher wanted to order for class work would be ordered.

After my retirement from Bexley, I continued to bring in my New Yorker magazines. On a winter's morning, as I made my way through the turnstile just inside the library door, I sensed the usual calm of the library had been transformed.

"Oh, you've brought more magazines..."

I could hear the voice, I couldn't see the owner of the voice. The tiny office, just beyond the head librarian's desk, was waist-high stacks of materials: books, folders, manuals, brochures, flyers. I still couldn't see the owner of the voice, but I thought I recognized LouAnn, the Library Assistant. "LouAnn, are you there somewhere?"

And from a small square I could see the top of LouAnn's hairdo.

"LouAnn, what are you doing in there????"

She looked a shade frantic, her usually tidy shirt and skirt somewhat dusted over.

"Oh," she said, "we have so many classes this winter. I'm trying to get ready for them."

When a class would arrive at the Library for a 43-minute research encounter, it was understood that the available books would already be assembled on a large cart. The accompanying teacher would say a few well-chosen, crisp remarks, translated "Shut up and work quietly. Find a book you can check out five minutes before the bell". The head librarian meanwhile would be casting a cool eye over the group: "Class, you are here to work. Young lady, what are you doing? Are you in this class?? (This to a chippie on the edge of things, who had suddenly found her boyfriend in the research tables ... the chippie would beat a retreat.)

Classes would come and go, preparatory to writing the term paper, or presenting a persuasive speech or giving a report on the life and times of Charles Dickens.

"LouAnn", I said, "I've brought the latest New Yorkers and a few leftover Smithsonians..."

"Thanks so much. You know, I am amazed at how many students are using the New Yorker these days"!

"Well, fine," I said. I didn't add that I thought I knew why the New Yorker had suddenly become so popular. With the new female editor, it had become a swinging new magazine. There were still some indepth political, social and economic articles, but the fiction was now ablaze with the "f" word and the sexual capers of the 90's. Even the ads and covers were campy and filled with scantily clad characters. The biographical articles had switched to personalities with more colorful pasts and less serious philosophy. I thought it somewhat surprising that the head librarian, who could only be described as aloof and good looking, would be tolerating so much New Yorker reading by persons under 18.

I concluded that she at least did not read the New Yorker ever. Actually, I had never come across a current librarian reading anything except the riot act to the students who had come in to find Sports Illustrated. When I had first been at Bexley in the 60's, there was a much smaller library, two librarians and one assistant, and all three were readers and researchers. If a student needed to know more about the worst polluted lake in the USSR, the latest book or magazine article on that subject would be recommended and waiting for the student to pick up at the end of day.

With the advent of the Library Computer System, one of the four librarians on duty would proclaim, "We can get you any book or magazine article you want from another school". Students began to complain that the Library didn't really have anything. Of course, sometimes, that simply meant they didn't have the current issue of Rolling Stone– Rolling Stone had the cut-off date posted on the magazine storage room door.

Well! The Rolling Stone certainly had nothing on the current New Yorkers. Come to think of it, I figured the changes in the New Yorker would not be noted for a long time to come: the teachers didn't do much current reading; the principals had never been serious readers, likewise none of the upper level admin staff; the head of the English Department who worked evenings in the paint store never was an enthusiastic reader, nor the Board Members, nor the Superintendent.

It has also occurred to me that some of the "school censorship" is rather like "broadcast censorship". When I was running a local talk show, no one, until the racial problems of the late 60's, really said you must not interview this or that person. We just kept in mind who the sponsors were, and we tread lightly over sensitive topics. Like teachers, our salaries were small, our perches precarious, and I don't believe there were any Edward R. Murrows amongst us. I was probably less intimidated as a teacher than I was as a broadcaster: teachers have tenure, broadcasters–local ones at least-can expect summary notice at any time.

But now, as I write this chapter and hear the news that the State Board of Education in Kansas just eliminated the mandate to include the teaching of evolution in the science curriculum, I realize there is something much more serious going on.

The real problem in censorship rests with those who fear books. A letter by Edwin Frownfelter appeared in our local paper some months ago. He said he was saddened to learn that somebody in our community was trying to abolish Ray Bradury's story, "The Veldt"–the reason given, because it encourages violence against parents. Mr. Frownfelter went on to say that thirty years ago he read everything by Bradbury and other writers of science fiction. Further, he said he would be delighted if his high school aged children were avid enough readers to find "The Veldt". He then pointed out that it is the business of science fiction to change the rules, discard assumptions we live under and explore what life would be like without them.

His closing line of the letter to the editor was: " Don't fear books; fear people who fear books."

How true. Violence will be in schools as in many other places. Theft will be in schools as it is in many other places. Our real problem is CENSORSHIP. Censorship strikes at the core of what a public school in a democracy should be: the place to find the truth, to debate all the viewpoints and known facts about a subject.

"Those who expect to reap the blessings of freedom must undergo the fatigue of supporting it."

-Thomas Paine

What Is A Strike Like?

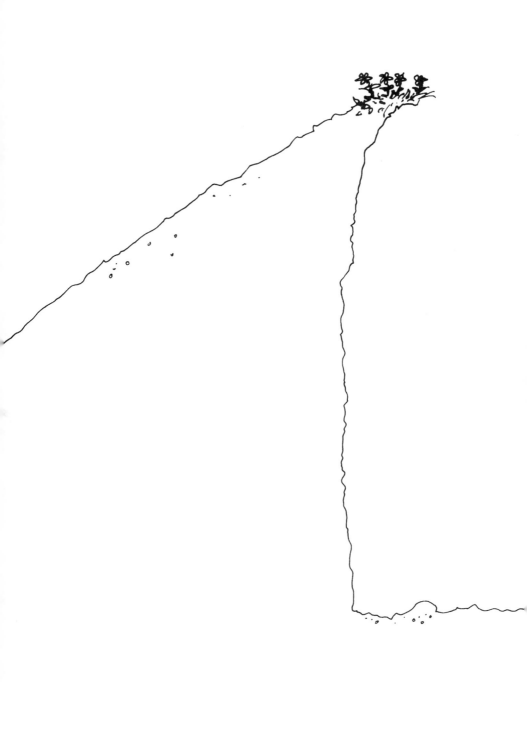

In 1984, an editorial in our local paper read: "PSEA Seeks Pie in the Sky". This editorial was motivated by the PSEA President's call for increasing the average teacher's salary by $12,000 over the next three years.

The writer asked: "If there is a direct correlation between higher salaries for teachers and improvement in the quality of education, somebody had better explain why educational levels have been declining for more than a decade in which teacher salaries rose as fast as in previous history". The writer continued–"We would agree that the average starting salary for teachers in Pennsylvania of approximately $13,000 is too low..."

You will perhaps remember in 1966 1 had begun at $5500; it took almost 20 years for the beginning teacher to reach $13,000.

In 1988, when our district struck, starting salary had reached $18,000, but South Shore had evaded paying this amount. They managed to PROMISE to pay and did not deliver, even after a teacher had already been working for 18 months. This was the "trigger action" for the strike.

The editorial writer had also said, "It takes a lot of gall or social blindness to demand pay increases of this magnitude at a time when nearly one out of every ten workers in our state is out of a job, and when a growing number of school districts are falling into financial trouble and becoming burdens of the state". This writer's history classes must have skipped the chapter on the values of free public education.

What Is a Strike Like?

By 1988, the tenor of editorials had not changed: Revise School Act to Punish Teachers Who Go Out on Strike; Children Are Pawns of the Teacher Strike; BETTER PERFORMANCE GETS BETTER WAGES: UNHAPPY TEACHERS SHOULD GO ELSEWHERE! The entire first week of our strike was mostly letters like this appearing on the editorial page. We often felt that the editor(s) had had some knuckle-smashing teachers, in the days when corporal punishment went unchallenged.

Actually, the letter about the children being pawns of the teachers was PRO-teacher and education. The writer asked who had lined up six Sub teen kids displaying anti-strike posters and lettered T-shirts purporting to show their view of the current delay in public school openings. (The headlines of letters were sometimes twisted.)

Life on the picket line began at 7 am, to assure a parking space off school grounds. Emerging from our cars, we untangled the twine on our signs, put on the walking shoes, and by 7:30 we were walking on the concrete.

The grass next to the sidewalk would have been kinder to the feet, but we were setting a good example: we walked on the concrete, three abreast at times, on the sidewalk only. Two blocks up the hill and two blocks down the hill. Hour by hour.

TV cameras came along. It was quite by accident (I think) that an announcer stopped by me. I am reasonably certain he didn't know what my previous occupation had been and—at what stations I had broadcast in years past. He was a young thing and eager to ask pertinent questions.

"What do you teach?"

"Communication", I answered.

"Oh. Well, why are you striking?"

"Our district believes in excellence for education. We want to attract and hold an excellent staff".

Or some such words to that effect. I must have sounded convincing because that bit of tape was run over and over–MONTHS later. Someone would see me in a store the following Spring and say, "I saw you again on TV! The local CBS station certainly got a lot of mileage out of that footage (pun intended).

Cars would go by. Often the occupants would yell obscenities. Once in awhile, perhaps one out of ten drivers, would give us a thumbs-up sign.

We walked on frosty September mornings. We walked until 3 pm in the Indian Summer afternoons. We walked in the rain. Fortunately, that was a fairly dry autumn—the heavens were kind and we didn't have many drenching days. My husband would drive by on his way to golf (he was already retired), and a cheerful honk and thumbs-up added to our support quota.

The day came when some of us were asked to volunteer to walk in front of the Administration building, two miles away from Bexley in one of the South Shore boroughs. The young teachers looked uneasy. A colleague and I, who had been there for 20 years, volunteered.

Our new strip of concrete was in a more visible place, at a busy intersection; it was a tighter sidewalk, with room enough for just two persons side by side. A rent-a-cop stood on the grass at the property, giving us perfectly vacant stares. The District Superintendent must have been ducking quickly in the rear door–he was never visible at the front door.

We walked and walked, robotic, silent, unsmiling. I remember I was wearing dark blue loafers; they lasted the length of the strike, but were permanently too enlarged to wear thereafter.

There was a committee to help those on the line. They brought food and beverage every two hours. It was very thoughtful of whoever appointed the committee to include Home-Ec teachers: with cheerful efficiency these creative women brought us luscious fruit and salad concoctions, delectable pastries and cookies–we ate well.

As we walked, we wore our signs. My large black and white sign declared: "ON STRIKE. South Shore Education Association "TEACHERS WHO CARE". "MAGIATRI IAMDUDUM DEFUTUTI SUNT" I saved my sign: in spite of rain showers, morning mist. A coffee smudge along the lower right hand side, it is still in good shape.

At Bexley Hills High, the only person to cross the line was the football coach. Even the Coca-Cola delivery-man did not enter the building. The other football coach from our sister school did not enter. Bexley's Coach later gave up eating in the teacher's dining room for several years. It was an interesting lesson in non-communication to note how his entrance would stop all conversation–we were all suddenly busy with the pizza buns or the spaghetti, digging into it furiously with our plastic forks.

What is a strike like? It was not only the newspaper editor who was unsympathetic to striking teachers. My husband and I were at our Club for dinner one autumn evening during the strike. An acquaintance (well, at least he wasn't a regular golfing partner) remarked to my husband, "You know, if I were head of that school district, not a goddamn one of those teachers would come back EVER."

I don't think the acquaintance knew where I collected my paycheck. I do not know what business he was in; like Janet of the Far Right, I did not want him for my Board Director EVER. But I would have thought that since he was deemed worthy of membership in what was the oldest and most respected club in the city, he might have troubled himself to learn at least what the issues were and be willing to discuss them, if not agree to them. A few months later, when my husband died of a heart attack at Christmas, I cancelled the Club membership on January 1.

A strike does let you know where your friends are. A week after the strike ended, without a settlement, twelve days after it had begun, I was seated at the hairdressers. I did not know the names of most of my hairdresser's other clients, but the lady waiting for her dye to take was saying," You know, can you believe those teachers?!?!!. What a terrible example for the students...."

The hairdresser suddenly raised the volume on his Christian Radio program, then was rapidly flipping stations, and the lady was somehow quickly whisked under a heat lamp with a People magazine thrust into her hand.

I had taught the son and daughter of my hairdresser. Perhaps Father feared a sudden altercation in his otherwise peaceful establishment. He need not have worried. Whoever the woman was, she, like the acquaintance at the Club, lived in a different world. Neither one had probably ever gone back to their public school after they had graduated. Perhaps they had not even attended PUBLIC schools; maybe their parents had paid the local Academy fee or enrolled them in one of the large parochial schools.

Should I have explained the issues in a quiet, reasoned tone?

We are resorting to a strike because South Shore District is not paying the legal starting salary–this fact has triggered the strike. We have walked for twelve days because in this region South Shore school taxes are the lowest of any, and we are falling farther and farther behind in commitment to our schools. We walk because the $1500 average raise proposed by the Board translates into $500 for some teachers and $2100 for others.

We walk to compact the salary schedule. What this means is that we would like to reach top salary earlier than 29 years. The Board wants to add additional years so that no one could ever reach maximum pay. We walk because six local districts are paying better salaries–why should any of the best and brightest teachers come to us?

And I could have added–only the extra-duty package is now fair as proposed by the Union. The football coach who crossed the picket line, and whose benefits were second only to those of the Athletic Director, was amazed to learn from me that it took 60 to 70 hours to put a play together, that in 180 days I had to add 30 days of work—at home, week-ends, after school—to prepare plays and contestants in speech and theatre.

For the lady's further edification, I should have said: We walk because the Superintendent's salary is $70,000; the average salary for teachers is not yet near $33,000.

What is a strike like? There were plenty of fact-finding sheets, public memos and interviews on TV. The famous quote from one of those interviews was from the Superintendent (the $70,000 one) who said, "We are not negotiating trust; we're negotiating salaries". To be sure, those teachers paid $1500 below the figure they were hired at knew a lot about that.

There was another unintentional quote—a message in a paycheck stub for extra-duty people: "The worst kind of mistake is the kind you don't learn from". I should have taken that to heart in all the years before when I received $250 per play. Sixty hours into $250 translates to $4.00 per hour, way below the guy who was hired to cut the grass.

What is a strike like? There was a steady snow of paper—Picket Line Postscripts, Lunch Line Leftovers, Bargaining Alert News, Directions from the District. The latter was printed with the District Office letterhead: "Excellence in Education—a South Shore Tradition."

What is a strike like? It is meetings—in churches, theaters, motel conference rooms, playgrounds—before, during and eight months AFTER the strike. Most important to remember is the fact that a strike is most likely to occur at a time and place in the history of a school district when the Board has a certain complexity of character. Translated, that means two or three members are close buddies and ready for a terrific ego trip, and the other five or six rarely turn out for meetings at all. I had had one of the Board members of the strike era as a former student. He was fun, he was imaginative. He created a "volcano" for his demonstration speech and blew a hole, a modest hole, in the floor at the rear of my classroom. He had entered local political eventually, was in real estate, and served on the Board to be better known. He surely had little interest in the tedium of weekly Board meetings.

What many strikers were amazed to discover about a strike was the A F T E R M A T H.

For the In-service Teachers' Program of 1990, three autumns after the strike, the District hired someone named John Popular to conduct useful workshops. That surely could not have been his real name—one would rather go through life as Hardy Feigenfelt or Fred Flurkey, than John Popular. Hardy and Fred I had had as students, so I understood about names.

Anyway, on a steamy summer weekend, sixty teachers, admin personnel and Board members traveled to a cooperation retreat with Mr. Popular. From the ensuing report on July 31, most of the teachers, admins and BM's who came to the Retreat were skeptical and apprehensive. "The first two days were not for everyone." But the writer of the report went on to say, "by discussing our problems we recognized that we had to start working together into the future, rather than rehashing the past. Goal setting was our vehicle to plan our commitment to work together. The 130 action plans were developed on the second day by four teams of teachers and administrators".

They had even developed a code language:

APP *Administrative Performance Plan*
BPC *Building Professional Committee*
CE(S) *Career Educators (Teachers and Admins)*
DCSD *Director of Curriculum and Staff Development*
OSC *Objective Steering Committee*
PR&R *(NOT the Pennsy Railroad of yore)*
Professional Rules and Responsibilities
TPAP *Teacher Performance Appraisal Plan*
(pronounced Tee Pap, not to be confused
with just plain pap)
SSSCC *South Shore Schools Cooperation Committee*

In the large bundle of materials strewn over my desk at the start of the 90-91 school year, I somehow missed the aqua page that held the key to this acronym, a by-product of the Retreat with Mr. Popular. Therefore, all during that year I found faculty meetings less and less comprehensible because much discussion was in code.

There was more than just p–p, of course, to the aftermath of the strike: there were 21 teacher transfers–the president of the Union, the line captains, the writers of the Picket Line Postscripts–all were transferred from high school to middle schools. A few teachers were allowed to return eventually to their original assignments. But during the next twelve years, the number of yearly district wide transfers rose from 21 to 73, the Superintendent's salary from $70,000 to 123,000, the administrative staff doubled, class size at Bexley increased by one-third.

So were all our efforts for nothing? No. As of the turn of the century, the starting salary is a respectable $34,000; the extra duty pay for a play, as an example, is $1500 our state which had been ranked 48th in terms of salaries and benefits is now ranked 5th in the nation. Still, editorials in the paper call for an end to teachers' right to strike, there are students who were never friendly to us again and. many parents who are to this day annoyed about our health benefits.

If you will now reread the preface of this book, you will also understand, sad to say, that the ethics of the system, (South Shore and many other public schools) is still quite skewed. Once a teacher reaches the maximum pay level, the strategy is employed to get rid of this too-expensive person. An unsatisfactory rating will be given, which freezes the salary. One of my former colleagues, only in her early 50's, still at Bexley, was given an unsatisfactory rating because she told a student his behavior was like that of a "Smart-A Kid". The student had refused to leave the classroom when the period ended; he was already disrupting the start of the next class.

Sometimes, however, the behavior of the Administrative staff and its Board, is such that it begins to destroy the power of its governing structure. What happened to South Shore in the 90's is another chapter of this book. My niece from South Jersey tells me that the same sort of situation happened in her district, so I do not feel that this has been a unique destruction on the part of South Shore. Perhaps over and over in history the pattern is repeated: Pride goeth before a fall.

Remember some of the lines by Carl Sandburg from his poem, "Four Preludes on Playthings of the Wind"?

And the wind shifts and the dust
on a doorsill shifts and even
the writing of the rat footprints
tells us nothing at all about
the greatest city, the greatest
nation where the strong men
listened and the women warbled:
Nothing like us ever was.

The Second Time Around

Not all parents reacted to their children's problems by writing a letter; there were those who showed up for a conference. In a track-two English class (a truly bizarre track-two English class) there was a strikingly beautiful red-haired girl. Tara (certainly aptly named) was bright, talkative, always in some kind of crisis situation, always in a rebellious state. I sent a progress report home; Mother shows up for a conference. Mother is tall, very blonde, very good looking."I certainly don't know what you're going to do with Tara", was her opening comment. "I don't think anything can be done with Tara. She is beautiful. She could be a model. She is impossible and always has been. Her father was an alcoholic. Don't know if you're aware or not–Tara is a latent alcoholic. In other words, if she drank anything, she would be an alcoholic. She's been to rehab twice. She never stops talking, she doesn't listen to anything I tell her. I do my best. She's not all like her brothers. And I've had problems recently. I'm divorced and my boyfriend just died. And now my new friend, the father of one of your other students–well, Tara can't stand him. I simply don't know which way to turn."

She gave me a long, long look, shifted slightly in her chair and finally said, "You know, when you had me in class you said I needed a muzzle."

I THOUGHT she looked familiar. I laughed what I hoped would sound like a good-natured understanding little laugh. She didn't chuckle, she didn't smile. She began talking again, mostly repeating what she had already told me. This time it was clear that it was not the current boyfriend

Tara hated–it was the son of the boyfriend–who sat across the aisle from her in English class.

Eventually, Tara's discomfiture was solved by the psychologist of the objectionable boy: contrary to school policy which prohibited any student from being transferred to another section after the fifth day of a new school year, the boy was allowed admission to another English class.

Other parents remembered me from earlier Bexley days when I had them in class. During my first months at Bexley, in the winter of 66-67, the classes were small and elective–speech was not a required subject in those days. In one class, a stocky, dark-haired, grumpy boy always sat off by himself. There was plenty of room for that–30 desks, 15 students–no need to crowd together. A counselor finally explained that the "boy" was almost 21 years old. When he turned 21, he'd have to leave. I don't recall his ever pre-senting a speech; he checked out before the end of the year.

Twenty years later, students like this boy were given far more attention, providing their parents allowed testing for exceptional traits. By 1986 I had each season at least one class of Learning Disabled students, or a combination of LD and Mentally Retarded students.

One day at the close of the period with the LD class, a stocky, dark-haired little girl stayed behind and remarked, "My Dad knows you. You had him in class a long time ago, and he's coming to Back to School Night."

"Melissa, that's good to know. I'll be very happy to see him", I said.

Back to School Night was South Shore District's major annual PR effort. On an autumn evening, scheduled so as not to conflict with the World Series, all parents were invited to come to school and follow the schedule of their sons and daughters on that particular cycle. (There were no "days" such as Monday through Friday; there were "cycles"' one through six). Parents had ten minutes for each class and refreshments in the Cafeteria during any Study Hall time. Teachers were to explain briefly the goals of the course; they were not to have any discussion about problems of any students. Just look professional, be POSITIVE, perhaps have a guest book all parents could sign. Show the text book used. GET ACQUAINTED!

I loved Back to School Night. Since I had been in broadcasting for seventeen years before I entered the teaching profession, Back to School Night was just like having my old Live-Audience-TV-Show: I wore my Burberry suit, had some fresh flowers on the desk, employed all my communication skills. And it did not take me more than one back to-school-night to notice that in a "good" section lots of parents showed up; in a section with "poor" students, almost nobody showed up. In Melissa's class, the LD section, there were three persons: one was Melissa's father. I spotted him right away. He was still dumpy, dark and scowling. (At least Melissa didn't scowl).

"You know," said he, "this here school ain't doin' nothin' for her."

"Oh, I'm sorry you feel that way," I said.

"They never done me no good, and they ain't doin' nothin' for her."

Remembering that we were NOT to get involved in particular problems, I said, "Well, Melissa seems to like this class. She's been presenting her speeches, and I believe she really enjoys being here."

"Huh" was all Dad said, and then he glanced at the schedule in his hand. He was due at the opposite end of the building for Gym Class in four minutes. With a final scowl he was gone.

Often it was in the competitive speech and theatre work that I met the sons and daughters of friends and even former classmates. On the evening of my 50th High School Class Reunion, an attractive, smiling woman who had been in my 9th grade Home Ec class, stopped at my table.

"Lil!" she said, "I've never had the chance to tell you this, do you realize you had both my son and daughter in plays and speech contests at Bexley Hills?"

Surely this fact had been the best-kept secret of my teaching career. I remembered the lady's name—Marian Wells. Wells? No, the children's name would be something else.

"I just can't remember your married name," I said.

She chuckled. "Jones," she said. "My son is Andy Jones, and my daughter is Ellen Jones. You'll remember—Andy was in "The Crucible", and Ellen won First Place in News Broadcasting at the State Tournament."

For the moment I just stared. I was still not connecting pleasant, low-profile Marian Wells with two of the most talented students I had ever coached. Andy was a superior actor. As Deputy Governor Handforth in "The Crucible" he brought fire and brimstone to the Salem witches' courtroom. (I also recalled that I was ready to fire him from the cast because of his delay in learning his lines.)

Both Andy and Ellen must have understood the concept of flextime years before flextime was put into practice. Ellen had a superb voice for broadcasting at the State Tournament her mother was recalling, I was also recalling that traveling with Ellen required much patience. If, for example, we were walking across the university campus to the broadcasting station, Ellen would pick up friends along the way, stop to chat and get further acquainted. It might be someone she had talked to briefly at breakfast, or perhaps a contestant from an earlier round. Never mind that we were still twenty minutes from the studio, that Ellen would have to take extra time to draw for position and then need still more time to prepare the newscast; Ellen was preoccupied with making a date with this newest acquaintance.

I would remind her that time was of the essence- Ellen actually liked such phrases–at least she liked the sound; the meaning did not speed her up.

Yet in all fairness to her style, she never missed an assignment. In the same style, she never missed rehearsals when she was in a play. She fell in an out of love with various leading male actors. Very often she was in two plays at the same time, yet her grades in all subjects remained "A's". I asked Marian what the children were doing now.

"Andy's an attorney in Washington D.C. He's married. Ellen has a doctorate in psychology. She married one of her professors. He's a bit older but we love him dearly. I really want to say 'thank you' for all you did for both of them."

We continued the reminiscence. I did not remind Marian of what turned out to be the most unusual trip I ever had with Ellen—and it involved her tournament broadcasting.

On the first day of her state competition, Ellen also had to appear in a one-act play at the Community Theatre. I had agreed to take her back to town for the play, then we would return to the tournament for the second day's schedule. It was a two-hour drive—no bad weather upstate in late April.

We started out from the university in good time, Ellen was chatting about a new friend she had just met—a boy from Pottstown: she had been in the audience for his dramatic reading presentation. By this time we were driving through a small borough—I was not noticing the speed signs—I assumed this was still a 55 MPH ZONE. Ellen stopped talking for a moment and then said,

"Mrs. J, I think the man in that car wants you to pull over." Indeed, as she said this I heard the low-toned siren, saw that a regional police car was on my left and that I should be pulling over. I pulled over, remembering at the same time that in the early morning rush to prepare for the tournament I had changed pocketbooks, so that now I would have no driver's license to show to the polite man who had just pulled me over.

It was soon established that I had been going over 10 miles per hour of the speed limit of this borough, that I would have until two days from now to take my driver's license to the Police Headquarters of the city, that I would be given points to work off in the Driver Refresher Course, held at my local high school. The polite policeman had no way of knowing, of course, that my local high school was where I taught, and that my refresher course would have an enrollment of sixteen truck drivers and me.

Finally, we were on our way again, and Ellen would be able to arrive at the theatre in time to participate in the play, "Interview". Then we would make a careful trip back to the state tournament. What I really wanted to ask Marian Wells, did you know early on you had such gifted children?

Thinking back to our Junior High days in Home Ec class—Marian had never shown much interest in plays, or debates. I don't recall that she was in any music group, nor did she end up editor of the newspaper, nor in the "top thirty" of the class that had 800 or so members. She was friendly, polite, attractive. I talked with her husband briefly at the Reunion—he seemed friendly, polite, and in his dark brown suit and striped tie he resembled the other recent retirees at their table.

I drove home from the Reunion, I was thinking that I had probably expected Mr. Jones to be more like Mr. Helstrom.

In our city, Mark Helstrom had become a legend in his own time. Actually, he was the youngest of the three Helstrom brothers—all three were legends in their own time.

They had emigrated from Norway right after WWII, had opened a chain and cable factory in our city and were very successful from day one. But it was not the business alone that created the legend. Each brother had a special talent, aside from making money in a fast growing business. The oldest brother was a musician (and composer), a violinist who was quickly urged to audition for the Mid-State Symphony; the second brother was a swimmer, holder of many medals; and Mark was an actor, who immediately found his way to the Community Theatre.

Early in the 1950's, our community theatre was fortunate enough to be moving into a newly built home of its own. "Lady In the Dark" was one of the first musicals to be performed in the new theatre. Mark Helstrom and I appeared in that show, not as leads, but with significant supporting roles. We sang a duet, in fact, with a certain amount of competence, as I recall.

Now fast-forward twenty years. In the first session of a September Speech class is a very blonde, very tall, very lovely Sophomore girl—her name is Anna Helstrom. I know at once who she is. Although Helstrom had already become a household name at Bexley (the eldest brother had eleven children, the middle brother, five), Anna was the first of Mark's progeny to attend our school. Anna was an actress; I was sure Anna would welcome contest work.

That particular season, we were also preparing to be the host school for the State Speech Association. We planned to do a Reader's Theatre version of "Summer and Smoke". This would be performed in a hotel conference room in center city on the first evening of the conference. Since it was a production which all of the delegates attended—theatre directors and instructors from colleges and high schools throughout the commonwealth—I had arranged for special lighting, music and sound effects.

We had presented a main stage production of this play the year before. The student playing John Buchanan, Jr. was now a Senior; the student who had played Alma Winemiller had already graduated. But here, to take her place, was another perfect Alma—Anna Helstrom.

I always encouraged parents to attend performances, even special "closed" events like that of the Speech Association. I was somewhat surprised, however, when Mark Helstrom showed up well before curtain time on the evening of the production. He asked to see the playing area, he asked who would be doing the lighting and music. I introduced him to the student technicians. Anna and the other cast members were still getting make-up and the stylized costumes that we used for Reader's Theatre production. Mark prowled to the far corners of the conference room (which would seat about 120 persons). The area for the players was slightly elevated, and since all the actors were on TV stools, I felt the sight lines would be good.

Now it was less than 25 minutes to curtain time.

"Mark", I said, "where would you like to sit in the audience? You have your choice before the delegates arrive..."

Mark pursed his lips. His hands were behind his back... He was twiddling his thumbs.

"I wish I knew more about the acoustics of this place
he finally said. "I have the feeling there are some really
DEAD spots." His brow was deeply furrowed.

"Well, the floor is carpeted and I've told all the cast
to think to the far wall. Even though it's Reader's Theatre,
they are in character all of the time. They have their
assigned line of vision above the audience on the wall
opposite. They actually look at the script very little... "

Mark broke in. "Still, it's a very difficult medium. I
certainly want Anna to be put at the best advantage."

By this time, I was not pleased with Mark Helstrom's
attitude, behavior, comments. I wanted very much to send
him back to his chains and cables. Too late for that–I had
invited him to see the performance, for better or worse.

I smiled warmly. I touched Mark's elbow and began
to steer him to an aisle seat, where I figured he would be
harmless to Anna. By now I didn't trust him not to do something really stupid, like noisily getting up and leaving in the
middle of the play, or shouting "LOUDER" if he' couldn't
hear, or talking out loud to the person next to him, explaining that Anna was his daughter.

On time, the lights dimmed, and after the musical
introduction, the play began. It rolled along as smooth as
satin to the close fifty minutes later, when there was exceptionally vigorous applause from the audience. From where I
was sitting, I could see that Mark did not join in. He was sitting with his arms tightly folded, in the kind of pose the communication textbooks always use to show that (a) the listener is angry or (b) the listener has a cold draft on his neck.

As the audience was leaving and the actors left to get changed, I began to clear the stage area, checking to be sure the technical equipment was being packed up. I noticed that Mark was still in his seat. Probably he was waiting for Anna, perhaps to give her a ride home. I had picked up all the students at school, had brought them down to the hotel in a van. At last Anna did emerge; I saw her going back to Dad. I was too far away to hear any conversation, but I could hear voices. In a couple of extra minutes, Mark's voice was getting louder...

"You don't really do yourself a favor by appearing in a space like this, Mark was saying.

I could not hear Anna's reply, and thought it wise to fade from the room. I was sorry for Anna, how could any father, even a fussy-pants, temperamental bundle-of-nerves father like Mark—be so insensitive as to treat a child with rude disrespect? Anna had presented an excellent performance. Even if Mark didn't appreciate the form of the play, or even the subject of the play, how could he refuse to thank her for a beautiful interpretation, how could he not find something kind to say?

Not at any time in the years I worked with Anna, in state competition, in main stage plays and play festivals, where Anna garnered a number of trophies—not ever did Mark thank me or even engage in any conversation about theatre, the School, the Community Theatre. By contrast, Mr. and Mrs. Jones turned out to be parents one could think of as role models for a gifted student. Perhaps a parent who is a legend in his own time cannot always be counted on for courtesy or a useful critique.

Sometimes a teacher's "second encounter" in the history of a family can take a very unusual twist. As with Jaime Galvez.

Jaime was an exchange student from Chile. More than that, he was our first exchange student from South America. The autumn when he arrived was a politically stormy time back in Chile.

During news discussions in class, Jaime would captivate the other students with his accounts of teen-agers in Chile, taking to the streets to lead the revolt against the corrupt government in power. Corrupt dictators we understood and surely sympathized with Jaime's desire for downfall of such a government, but we were very doubtful that a military takeover would solve the problem. How, we often asked him, are you going to get the military out of power and have free and democratic elections? Jaime replied optimistically (naively, we privately thought) that democracy would come in time. Time was what was needed.

Not all exchange students were as vocal nor half as interesting as Jaime. Our exchange student from South Africa, for example, who spoke perfect English (she was not of Dutch background–English–she assured us), would never discuss anything except the flora and fauna of the beautiful land of South Africa. All our questions about apartheid were graciously put aside–flora and fauna took over.

At the close of the year with Jaime Galvez, we said good-by, and he insisted that we all write down his home address in Santiago–should we ever happen to come down to Santiago, we should please come round to visit. All nineteen of us in the class promised, and carefully wrote down our own addresses to send along with him.

Twenty-one years later, the first winter of my retirement, we had our first big snow storm in mid-December. Twenty inches of snow was far too much volume for my small electric snow blower. Forget the snow blower, just keep shoveling in one-hour shifts. A white sculpture of a car was in the driveway. Best perhaps to start with the car: use a broom for the top, a brush for the windows–maybe not, since the brush was still inside the car with the doors not even visible. I worked at an even pace and after the first hour, the car was slowly emerging.

The street had been plowed, and across the chunks of snow at the end of the driveway I saw that a car had stopped, not a neighbor's car–this was a handsome Mercedes, gleaming in the sun and snow. The driver had just got out of the car and was coming up the driveway, briskly too, in spite of the heavy snow.
"Mrs. J!" he shouted.

I put down my shovel, still wondering whose friendly voice this might be, when the person's face, as handsome and gleaming as the car, suddenly came into focus–JAIME GALVEZ!

"Jaime, hello! What are you doing here in all this crazy snow???"

"I am here in time for Christmas with my host family. I want you to meet my own family right down here in the car..."

And then I was being introduced to a stunning

young woman, who was holding the one-year-old daughter. The middle child was also a girl, and the boy was about seven or so.

"Now Mrs. J, my son and I will do your shoveling. And me ... I will help!" This from middle child, the daughter who was three? maybe four??

By this time I was opening the front door for Jaime's wife and the baby. Jaime already had the shovel, Jaime's son the broom, and middle child was brushing the car windows.

I was soon to learn from Dolores, Jaime's wife, that Jaime was now a judge in Santiago. This was the first time in two years that they'd been able to get away to visit for Christmas, and Jaime was very anxious to visit all of his teachers and to stop at the school if the principal would permit. Jaime would like to speak to some of the students, especially those who might be going to study law eventually, or consider a political career. And then Dolores was handing me a bag of Chilean candies, rather like our toy candy treats.

I never did have a chance to ask if ever there was snow in Santiago. I couldn't ever remember seeing a picture of anything like a wintry Santiago. We had always talked politics with Jaime. I had never been to anywhere in South America—our trips were always to somewhere in Europe.

There were tons of questions I wanted to ask, but already Jaime and his crew had the drive opened and were ready to look up the next teachers.

"Remember, Mrs. J, you did promise. If you ever come down to Santiago, you must look us up. We would so like to have you visit!"

"The years teach much which the
days never know"

-Ralph Waldo Emerson

Main Stage Magic

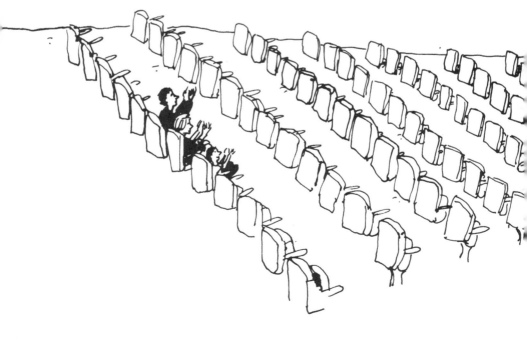

"Mrs. J..." Ron's voice was intense, almost pleading. "We want you to be the director."

Ron's carrot red hair somehow added to the intensity of his request.

"I'm not sure, Ron. I certainly am pleased to be asked, but I'm not sure Mrs. Grant thought of me as director for the main stage."

Actually, I suspected Mrs. Grant guided other faculty members to the Main Stage and had purposely avoided the main stage herself, with its long evening rehearsals and six weeks of set-building and costume-piecing-together.

"Mrs. J!" Ron's voice rose higher as he pushed his glasses back up on his nose. "We want to do Up The Down Staircase. You know, it's from the book by Belle Kauffman, and there's a whole roomful of kids–it's a large enough cast. The Principal reminds me of..."

Ron was about to say "Mr. Anderson", our diamond-in-the-rough. I cut in quickly.

"Ron, I'm also not sure how the play will be accepted here. There might be some staff who find it a put-down on the school. "It's FUNNY, Mrs. J, it's a SCREAM...IT'S SO COOL!!"

I was thinking of some other recent main stage productions. "Our Town", "The Dark at the Top of the Stairs", "The Mouse that Roared", "Picnic"–all much "safer" than the message of "Up the Down Staircase". In fact, even "Picnic had its detractors: Miss Wehler, head of the English Department, in her paper whispery voice had confided to me at one lunch time, "I really think the teacher is degraded. I find her so embarrassing."

If Miss Wehler found it impossible to laugh at her-self, or cry with sympathy for a compatriot, I could not con-ceive: that Mr. Anderson would be even minimally amused by a caricature of himself. At the same time I was thinking that Ron could do that role excellently–the medium-size potbelly, shirt hanging out over, the round shiny face with the glasses always sliding down the nose.

Ron was a Senior, an actor from an acting family. The son of a middle-school teacher and a nurse both long-time performers at the Community Theatre, Ron had an older brother who was already in New York City playing in Off-Broadway productions. In other words, Ron's family was respected in the South Shore community. I would be point-ing out to Mr. Anderson that "Up the Down Staircase" was the students' request, that Ron spoke for their choice.

Already in many high schools there were protests against the Viet Nam War; there were underground news-papers and sit-ins. What with Dr. Martin Luther King Jr.'s death and the assassination of Bobby Kennedy in recent months, I was thinking, Mr. Anderson, you are a very, very lucky principal–your students simply want to stage "Up the Down Staircase". My, oh my yes, you are lucky!

We were almost three weeks into rehearsal when I realized we were not knitting"–my own term for the weaving of a production. The 23 students had yet to realize they were not to play themselves; they were to create characters and perform as a team. They were not a team, not even a scrub team. Attendance was good. That was all that was good.

In the middle of the eighth rehearsal, Ron abruptly faced the group. And he wasn't the Principal, he was Ron himself, taking charge as a Director.

"Look you guys. We want this show to be something our class is proud of. You're not doing anything right, and you know it. You must learn the EXACT lines. You must come here prepared to be the character you are, play that a person all the time you're here. YOU DON'T SCREW UP! If you can't agree to do that, you can leave right now".

All 23 were quiet. As quiet as the dark-at-the-top-of-the-stairs. All 23 were believing every word Ron was saying. They respected him.

These were not the select, competitive actors. This cast had to learn fast that a play was not a "joke", that to be truly funny in a role required tremendous concentration. I had incorrectly assumed they already knew that. When I had directed In-Company Musicals, actors were about ten years older than Seniors, and they were anxious to impress their supervisors. The high school senior must impress his peers, at least satisfy his peers, who are his "supervisors" socially.

After Ron's diatribe, we made remarkable progress in pulling the show together. The set was a delight: heads could pop out of the wall, rather like a worm popping out of a teacher's apple. If Mr. Anderson had any misgivings about his stage image, he at least maintained a "good sport" façade.

There were two performances, with every seat filled both evenings. A total of 2400 persons from student body and community saw the show and loved it. Except for one frosty senior girl who said the play was more related to Junior than Senior High school. Ah well, she was ahead of her time, unfortunately.

That was the first main stage play I directed at Bexley, in the Autumn of 1969. About 50 plays later, in 1993, the last main stage play I directed was Neil Simon's "Plaza Suite".

What kind of acting space did the main stage at Bexley provide? Built at the end of the 50's, Bexley expected to have a student enrollment of 1400 at the most. Before the school was finished, the population of the district had shifted somewhat–there were 1800 students ready for enrollment. The auditorium, in contemporary tones of teal and shrimp, seated 1200; there was a need for double assemblies right from the start.

The stage was HUGE, the apron very generous. But the architect was not thinking theater: there was no fly space (translated this means a low ceiling, with klieg lights requiring all available space above the stage); very limited wing space–the areas off stage right and left were so snug only very small wagons (the portable stage units on rollers, holding scenic pieces to allow for quick set changes) could glide in and out; there were no dressing rooms, no set building areas behind the back stage wall.

Clearly the architect was thinking Christmas concert, Awards Assembly, Baccalaureate Service, what with the ample orchestra pit holding a Steinway grand piano AND an organ. For the baccalaureate event the entire hierarchy of Board members, the minister, rabbi, and priest, the eighty-voice choir, the officers of the class—all could be seated quite comfortably on the stage.

Now downsize to a PLAY of the mid 20th century. We did encourage large cast plays, but even a fine old chestnut like "The Man Who Came to Dinner" had only thirty or so cast members, including maid, butler and broadcasting crew. And as the century rolled along, plays by leading playwrights had even smaller casts: "The Glass Menagerie" by Tennessee Williams, a cast of four; "All My Sons" by Arthur Miller, a cast of ten.

Much of our focus on staging involved techniques to shrink visually the stage space: securing a full set of black stage curtains (that same architect always recommended non-useful beige curtains); building stairways and low platforms, so that a pool of light could tighten an acting area. Or, as in the case of Thornton Wilder's "The Matchmaker", transform in ten seconds Mrs. Malloy's hat shop into an elegant New York City restaurant.

This play, you may remember, became the beloved musical "Hello, Dolly". We produced "The Matchmaker" in the mid 70's. It was a great choice—large cast, colorful sets, handsome RENTED costumes. There was just one pitfall: there were hundreds of props, from picture hats to potted palms, and it was not the kind of play where you could simplify, and then simplify some more. The fun was in all the colorful THINGS as well as the eccentric characters.

Sometimes, the gods are kind to a director. As it turned out, my daughter Vicki was cast in the role of Mrs.

Malloy. Early on in rehearsal she noticed all was not well with the props. At this point we were still using substitute items.

After one particularly confusing session, Vicki came to the back of the auditorium where I was balancing note pad and flashlight, scratching down what I thought might untangle some of the hat store snarl-up.

"Mom, it's just not going to work this way. We need something or someone, just beyond the doorway Up Right. Someone has to be sorting and sifting, and when the restaurant..."

"Vicki, can you think of anyone from the restaurant scene who would be in costume already, and have time to be at that doorway for about 20 seconds or so...?"
"Maybe...it just might be LEN!"

"Yessssssss–Len, the young male lead. Len had a special skill for organization, not people particularly, but PROPERTIES. Len would be so good at making lists, assigning cast members to show up with what was assigned, plotting little places behind the set so that all of these objects–large, small even fragile–would show up on stage in the right scene at the right time. Len's skill did not end with lists. He could dance and act, and he was so good looking. Len does not come along often, even in a school of 1800 people. When he does, one can stage "The Matchmaker", and this memo will go to every member of the cast on Opening Night. Opening Night memos are a kind of "good luck note", instead of saying "break a leg", the traditional quip before curtain time.

Lillian Juditz

Memo

You're surprised? You're surprised we
finally get this show together. Well now,
after six weeks of confusion and hard work
we have the right to a little risk and
adventure_ (Opening Nights held PLENTY of
risks.) And another thing about an Opening:

Remember, 99% of the people in the world
are AUDIENCE, and the rest of us are on
stage (which is certainly foolish of us,
but fun nonetheless).

Indeed, isn't Opening Night full of
wonderful things? It's nothing like dress
rehearsal, with potted palms upstaging you,
purses missing, doors not shutting.

Opening Night is so different. You feel
like laughing-hysterically.

I pity the person who's never had the
pleasure of an Opening Night. The feeling
of your stomach tied in a knot, the chill
of your dear wee hands and feet.

Obviously, Opening Nights are not for those
who have the soul of a field mouse, nor
for those who wish they were at home where
nothing ever happens.

Everybody keeps asking me if we're ready
for tonight. So what's to get ready???
Only 17 actors and 700 props. The only
thing we DON'T have is the Mayor of New
York!

So, ladies and gentlemen, may I make a
suggestion? For those of you who are
unduly apprehensive about an Opening
Night-here is the advice of a Director: It
looks to me, like what with all the crew
flying in and about and everybody acting
so, so strangely...Ohhhhhhh...HELP!!!!
THERE'S AN AUDIENCE OUT THERE......I'VE NEVER
SEEN SUCH A NIGHT!! LORD SAVE US!!!!!!!!

(That's the opinion of the first Mrs. Juditz)

For the reader who has never seen "The
Matchmaker", nor read the script, the memo is a parody on
the philosophy of Horace Vandergelder, the rich old mer-
chant of Yonkers, the older male lead in the play.

In a much earlier chapter, I had mentioned no
"Principal's Committee" had ever been appointed to tell me
which plays to present and which to avoid. I was free to
choose. My first consideration was always: is this material
worth working on for six weeks, will I want to watch this play
from the back of a chilly auditorium for at least forty times,
will I still love it or come to hate it?

For a classic like "The Crucible" (Arthur Miller), this criterion was no problem; it was not as much a given for "All My Sons" (also Arthur Miller), probably because the language of the play lacks the beauty of "The Crucible". Which brings up another consideration: I had to be sure the potential actors for a play were more or less equally adept at handling the language. For example, Agatha Christie's "Witness for the Prosecution" probably represents the playwright's finest craft; the language is superior. It is so superior I realized, about two weeks into rehearsal, that some of the actors were bewildered by it. The problem could be remedied only by many extra small scene rehearsals.

Which brings up consideration number three. Do the actors available for this play have good voices, interesting voices even? We can rely on all kinds of tricks to make actors LOOK right. To SOUND right, the actors have to come to us with that talent already in place.

Still more criteria for choosing the play: during the three or four years students are with us, let us make sure they see contemporary plays as well as classics, comedy and tragedy, farce, satire, plays based on a true story, mystery plays. And if we ever repeat a choice, let us be sure it has not been done in the past dozen years.

I can hear readers thinking what about cost, what about a too-complicated set, what about the problem of costuming? One important point to remember about economy: in terms of royalty expense, all non-musicals are very modest in price. Fifty dollars for the first performance, thirty-five for the second. Sets? As to the materials part, sets are built and rebuilt and rebuilt ad infinitum from much of the same lumber. For a time at Bexley, we had very willing and able set building crews and expert faculty leadership. When these faded I hired outside help and personally financed this for a time until the Principal of that era asked me, "Why do you want to do this?" I told him I believed in this work and its value to the students. I surmised he didn't think it was a wise way to finance school theatre; it was at that point the changing fortunes of the Student Council brought forth new funding, via management of the vending machines.

As to costuming, I would scout yard sales for unusual smoking jackets, eveningwear, uniforms. Older female members of my family gave their handsome wool knits and furs to me instead of Goodwill. My husband gave his shoes. Shoes made of leather, with ties; even leather loafers were almost non-existent in students' wardrobes. I sent actors to Goodwill to find value-priced vintage clothing and large size mens' three-piece suits. Early on in my directing career I learned a lesson about large sizes. We needed a size 48 conservative suit for a portly father figure. One of our track coaches looked like a 48 to me. I asked at lunch one day, would he happen to have a suit, that he had saved, that we could borrow, that we would take very good care of...we needed a size 48, or thereabouts, I added. First, there was a cool stare. Then as he was attacking his second steak roll, between bites he mumbled, "No. No. I wouldn't have anything like that". The cool stare turned to frost. Other play-choice considerations? Timeliness. We did an adaptation of Orwell's "1984", in '84. Wilder's "The Skin of Our Teeth" in 1976, the Bicentennial year. "The Diary of Ann Frank" on the 50th Anniversary of the writing of the diary.

Familiar titles brought in more audience, but I also chose to do the unfamiliar "Brown Pelican" (by George Sklar) because of the environmental message. Of all the fifty main stage plays I directed, that was the only one for which I received a special request six years after we presented it. The message was from a graduate student at the University of Miami. A former graduate of Bexley had told him about this play, he wanted to use some material from the play for his thesis presentation. Could I please send him a copy or tell him where to secure the script? One just never knows how far a message can travel.

Awhile back I said that in staging a play our big problem was how to use all that enormous stage space. In the mid-80's I had an inspiration. We would put AUDIENCE on the stage, too, for "Theatre Up Close, There were risers available from the choral department. We would have three-sided theatre-just one wall—with the audience on three sides. It was a beautiful, fantastically workable arrangement.

We sailed through "My Three Angels", "The Dining Room", and almost, almost we made it harmlessly through "Absurd Person Singular" (A. R. Gurney, Jr.) Almost, until Peggy Lansing's mother fell into the orchestra pit midway through Act Three.

Like Ron of "Up the Down Staircase", Peggy was from a performing arts family. There had been six children.

Two boys, four girls. The boys were musicians, the oldest girl was a dancer, and the three younger sisters were actresses. Both parents were enthusiastic audience at all plays, concerts, and musicals.

On the second evening of "Absurd Person Singular" however, Sheila Lansing, Peggy's mother, was attending the play by herself. Her seat was on the third level of the risers, downstage side. Often during the play I could hear her infectious laughter. From my seat on the inner stage right, I could also see Sheila's head turn occasionally to the person on her right. Until well into the Third Act.

About Two-thirds of the way through this act, there is a partial blackout. In the script, the two couples in the scene are aware that a third couple (two persons they don't like very much) have just reached the back door to their kitchen. The "inhospitables" reason that if they switch off the lights, the "unwelcomes" will go away. Probably when the lights were squelched, Sheila had adjusted her chair a bit, not noticing in the dim light that she was too close to the rear edge of the riser. I heard the scraping sound of the folding chair, then a softly thumping sound, as the late-arriving couple in the play pushed right into the kitchen. The host brought the lights back up.

At that point I knew the extent of our crisis: Sheila was no longer visible. Already Mr. Thomason of the faculty, who was on duty that evening as a chaperone, was already climbing down into the pit to assess Sheila's condition.

I could hear some crisp directions. A student usher was heading for the nearest exit and the hall phone to dial

911. "Absurd" was still going on. I was thinking very fast–should I stop the play?–there were still four minutes to the end. The audience, except for about three persons from Sheila's row, were all watching the play and laughing in the appropriate places. The players, including Peggy Lansing, apparently had not realized at all what had happened. Two more minutes to go. There is no dialogue in the play at this point–simply the absurd pantomime of the game the six characters are playing. Fifteen seconds...

And now the play is finished. The audience, still laughing is applauding vigorously. The players are ready to take their curtain call as the lights are coming back up. There is another burst of applause. By now I can see Sheila rising unsteadily with the aid of Mr. Thomason; she is shaking her head a bit. As the audience is clearing, the EMS attendant is coming through the rear doors of the auditorium. A few minutes later I learn from Mr. Thomason that Sheila does not seem to have suffered any broken bones, that she probably has a slight concussion and that she is now on her way to the hospital to be examined.

I have no memory of how I cleared things away–the small props, make-up, costumes–the fake kitchen that was the set would be cleared away by the builder on Monday morning. No doubt I did finish up by 11 pm, the usual time to clear the building. But my mind was racing with all the 'what if' thoughts: What if Sheila does have a serious head injury? What if she is hospitalized for weeks? What if she SUES?–the school, the district? Meeeeee??????

By nine o'clock the next morning, Sunday morning, I reasoned that in spite of Church, Sunday School, whatever –somebody at the Lansing home might be able to tell me something–I could not endure the suspense any longer. I called. And Sheila herself answered. She was APOLOGIZ-ING, And saying it was just a slight concussion and not to worry. She was perfectly all right and she had enjoyed the show!

I said goodbye and hung up, and I thought, "Mrs. J, how could you be so lucky, and how many of your nine lives do you suppose you have left?" Finally, I wondered if Mr. Hoover would add this incident to his files.

Well, that was the short run of "Theatre Up Close".

Why had I been so anxious to have "Theatre Up Close", aside form the advantage of using all that stage area? Our audiences were now averaging 100 persons a night, in an auditorium that seated 1200 you will remember. So where had all the audience gone?

One obvious answer–when I arrived at Bexley there was an 1800 student enrollment, grades 10 to 12. By the 1990's, the enrollment was 1150, grades 9 to 12. When I arrived in 1966, about 10% of the students had part time jobs; when I left, about 80% had jobs, some of these were almost full time jobs. There were additional sports–golf, tennis, swimming for girls and boys. And for boys especially, soccer, as well as an enormous surge of interest in wrestling.

About half of the Bexley families were now frac-tured, meaning a single Mom was in charge of the family, or by contrast, there were two sets of parents, along with four sets of grandparents, all expecting to be visited on a regular basis. In one case, the student's father, whom he visited frequently, lived on the west coast.

Still, an analytical member of the Drama Club defined the problem of audience from a perspective other than time limits: it was no longer cool to go to a play. Rock concerts were still cool. Most any sports event was cool. Movies, some of then, were still cool, but too expensive—so rent the video instead.

The Drama Club analyst did not pursue the reasons for the change of cool, but recently, almost two decades after plays must have become non-cool, I was looking at the yearbook of 1967, and then at the yearbook of 1993. In '67 the entire first quarter of the book was devoted to plays, the musical, the musical organizations. Sports were about two-thirds of the way back.

In 1993, all the sports were up front, along with the homecoming queen and her court, the White Christmas Formal, proms. Most of the cultural activities were in the yearbook supplement, along with Commencement. I could certainly understand the rationale for Commencement in the supplement—it was not possible to present a detailed graduation ceremony and have it printed in time for the release of the yearbook. But a play which took place in December? Children's Theatre, in mid-winter? The latter didn't make either book, and yet the children who saw those plays in their elementary school is where the forthcoming students at Bexley were enrolled.

Does "cool" evolve, or is "cool" carefully engineered and marketed, depending who sits in the yearbook editor's seat? No Drama Club member had mentioned either, but I surmised another problem to do with "cool" was the division within the student body, as to "heads" and "straights" (drug users and nondrug users). One year there were separate after-prom parties to allow for this divisiveness. There was also the division along socio-economic lines, which resulted in cliques. Often mispronounced "clicks", nonetheless the cliques were set in concrete.

My mother had some ideas of her own about slim audience. She had been a very faithful playgoer from 1970 to 1985. From '75 on, she quite frequently would state, rather loudly at times, "Where are the teachers?"

Well, there were always at least two in attendance—they counted as chaperones", appointed by an Assistant Principal. There was no problem at all securing two "volunteers" for this assignment—no problems of vandalism, traffic control, or clean-up to worry about. Unlucky Mr. Thomason, who had to deal with the crisis of Sheila Lansing landing in the orchestra pit, was the only chaperone for a play who ever had to meet a challenge. I confess I found it hard to understand why teachers on their own did not want to enjoy a well-performed play free of charge. Plays by Neil Simon, Arthur Miller, William Inge, Tennessee Williams, William Gibson, Woody Allen, John Patrick, Beth Henley, Lillian Hellman, Noel Coward, Thornton Wilder, A.R. Gurney, Jr........

Until the mid-80's, musicals continued to draw big audiences. Then, to compensate for the dwindling evening crowds, we added a special Wednesday Matinee for the retirement homes of the community, along with a Wednesday MORNING "early bird" show for the older elementary school children. I helped stage a dozen musicals; I would have willingly stopped at the 9th or 10th, but on the last night of "Anything Goes", Anna Mae Stevens (from the chorus) stopped me in the hallway as I was gathering a miscellany of costumes, damp paper towels, a shoe or two. Anna Mae, without her glasses and still in make-up, looked quite nice really—almost unrecognizable from her daily school face.

"Oh Mrs. J!" she gasped. "It's been just super. I wish it could go on forever!" And she hugged me.

Anna Mae will never know that I endured the cutting critiques from a feisty little music director for two more musicals, just because I figured there were other Anna Maes out there, not very attractive girls, often overlooked for elections and queens' courts, for whom the main stage magically put them in an exciting world, where they were watched appreciated, applauded.

Perhaps if we had papered the bulletin boards and all the show posters with this little quotation by Françoise Hardy, we would have added some audience.

"There are so many dreams beyond
your night, and so much sunshine
behind your grey walls. But you
can't see it because you stay at
home. There is so much sky above
your roof. Is your door so old it
won't open, or are you staying at
home because you're afraid of
catching a chill?"

Driven by Dreams

Graduates at Bexley always processed into the stadium to the refrain of Elgar's "Pomp and Circumstance", until the year when a national brewery chose to use "Pomp and Circumstance" as the background music for their TV commercial showing kegs of beer bouncing along into summer.

Our graduates that June evening had to adjust to "Ode to Joy". The band director made no allowance for increased tempo. The musicians whipped along with Beethoven fervor, the grads in forced march struggled to stay five paces apart. The day's 90° temperature lingered on as the ceremonies got underway at six o'clock.

Actually it would have seemed appropriate to use the "beer commercial". Many members of the audience arrived wearing informal attire–jeans, a rumpled shirt, work shoes.

With large cigar in mouth, these friends and relatives would station themselves along the chain link fence that separated the bleachers from the field, flicking ashes through the links.

Since the sign at the stadium entrance declared, NO ALCOHOLIC BEVERAGES PERMITTED IN STADIUM, one had to assume no friend nor relative had brought along any cooling refreshment. One could not be quite sure, however.

The ceremonies continued for about two hours, and as the sultry spring evening wore on there were often cheers and special greetings as students' names were called during the awarding of diplomas,. "Yeah LOU ANN!" "Attaway to go Harry!" "Hey Debbie, I LOVE YOU! You're GORGEOUS!!!"

Despite the informality of the audience, the graduates, often numbering as many as 500 or so, were remarkably restrained (meaning well-behaved), until 1976. In 1976, for the first time, I was in charge of the speakers, which fact had nothing to do with the exploding fireworks and general rowdiness of the graduating seniors. It was, of course, the Year of the Bicentennial.

But I'm ahead of my story. Our daughter Vicki graduated from Bexley in 1975 during a week of heavy rains. There were two other faculty members with graduating progeny, and the three of us began to wonder if the gods had conspired: 1975 was to be the first year in the history of the school that commencement exercises had to be turned indoors.

Transferring a ceremony to indoors sounds mundane enough, but on a June evening of pouring rain, with no air conditioning nor workable windows in auditorium or gymnasium, the atmospheric effect was like a sauna. Each wilting graduate was allowed two family tickets to the ceremony in the gym. All the other relations, even from families numbering up to 15 or more, were relegated to the auditorium. To be sure, these people had softer seats, but the closed circuit TV of the mid-70's had reception that looked a lot like the torrential rain outdoors.

I can remember my mother and the in-laws from North Jersey peering as through a 'glass darkly.'

Faculty member Louis Sutton, who had been the coach of commencement speakers for at least a dozen years, also had a daughter graduating. Though we had no inkling that evening of the times ahead, the 1975 Graduation was to be more of a milestone than any of us realized. It would be the last commencement for Principal Anderson–ill health would give him early retirement; it would be the final time for Louis coaching the speakers–Louis would suffer a fatal heart attack a few months later, while escorting a student tour in Russia.

I had always sat in on graduation speech rehearsals. In fact, Louis had a relaxed, informal kind of communication feedback for the speakers: anyone who happened by was asked for comment. The custodian mowing the turf, members of the track team putting in a few practice rounds, the wash-up crew come to scrub the bleachers, the second Assistant Principal seeking a student who had escaped the Detention Room.

Traditionally, there were always four speakers at a Bexley Commencement. One to represent the Faculty, one to represent the Students, and the other two persons were selected from the Speech Department to represent, in Louis' opinion, effective Commencement speaking. Louis felt that frequently the faculty and students overestimated the speaking ability of their favorite candidates; therefore the Speech Department Seniors, fresh from regional and state competition would balance the presentation.

In 1975 the speakers' theme was "What Is Man?" The subtopic for each speaker answered one part of the question: the Faculty Speaker (who was also the Class Valedictorian...) explained "forged by the past"; the Student Speaker (who on his final day of classes had been seen "streaking" past the Principal's office window) would elaborate on "lonely with doubt"; the Speech Department students, my daughter (Class Salutatorian who had been presenting persuasive speeches all year on the American Indian Movement) would explore "driven by dreams" and the young man who had fended a barrage of questions about the U.S. Constitution for both American Legion and VFW oratorical events) would conclude the thoughts about man with "uplifted by hope".

It was an interesting contrast in acoustics–the stadium vs. the gym. Whereas in the stadium, where we had practiced for a number of sunny days, there was an echo from east to west-the length of the field; now, driven indoors to the gym, the echo extended from north to south–from rafters to the floor. Outdoors there would have been an occasional dog running by, the evening US Mail helicopter chopping by, and wind rushing through the microphone. Indoors there was steam, an occasional water bug suddenly visible from the shower rooms beneath the gym, and the pervasive phys-ed aroma permeating the clothing of the 1500 persons gathered together.

When it was Vicki's turn to speak on that memorable evening, this is what she said:

"Someone asked the famous painter Matisse, just what was his inspiration? Matisse replied, I grow artichokes. Every morning I go into the garden and watch these plants. I see the play of light and shade on the leaves and I discover new combinations of color and fantastic patterns. I study them.

Then I go back into the studio and paint." Now obviously, not everyone feels this way about artichokes, and the reason is that there are two ways to look at the world, two perspectives.

One is to see the world in a cut and dried form, to believe in facts without wondering why they exist or whether they could change. Many of us will admit only to this dimension of life. We are content with a humdrum existence, with following well-worn ruts that we never break out of simply because it's easier not to. We tend to look at the so-called great men—the Shelleys, Debussys, Rousseaus and feel terribly inferior—so much so we feel mediocrity is the best we can do. We fail to realize that a higher plane of thought lies within our grasp.

This higher plane or second perspective involves looking beyond concrete surfaces to abstracts, finding new facets to common objects—appreciating their beauty and form. To master the second perspective is to see what others do not, never to see a thing without seeing another beside it, or behind it. To attain this you must not only see, but observe; not just hear, but listen; not simply absorb, calculate, and regurgitate but let your mind wander into mazes of imagination, set it free.

Children have this gift before the adult world stifles it. They pretend to live with the rest of us, and we think that their lives are mere reflections of our own. But in reality, they are as self-contained as cats—creating a secret, magical world of their own. To them life is an adventure—every lamppost or oak tree, every colored scarf or painted butter-

fly—acts as a transparency to a myriad other forms. A life-time of dreams and promises compacted into a few feet of infinite space.

But soon imitation takes over; the child begins to copy the gestures, the manners, the thought patterns of adults. His brimming wealth of interest and questions and amazement ebbs away. He goes to school, allows other people's thoughts to replace his own and smother his creativity; once out of school he makes money or arrives or just amuses himself—imagination is only a word. In short, the outcome is the exact opposite of what it should be—we travel steadily away from thought, and the process begins when we are six years old.

But through a conscious effort we can regain the essence of the second perspective, of the higher plane of thought. The mind is an ocean. In its deepest currents flow the fragmented crystals of creation. A little rain, a summer storm, can bring them to the surface for an instant, and can give us a glimpse of whole regions of the mind so different from our daily thought.

There was a cyclist caught in a thunderstorm. He was forced to pull over and wait it out, and in that short period he was forced to look around him, really look. He saw things he had never seen before. As the rain passed, a mist-softened landscape materialized before him—a landscape of new colors and contours. He discovered the fluffy cream of dandelions gone to seed, the eerie gray of cloud shadows on the hills, the soft bluegreen line where the trees melt into the sky. Just the countryside after rain, and yet a novel experience. There was a certain something which changed the ordinary into the exotic and fascinating, and all because he took time to feel and observe in a different dimension, from a different perspective.

It is not difficult to reach the second perspective-but it requires determination and a little courage, a little courage to move over a line and escape the ruts of conformity. Our opinions of other people all stem from ourselves; we see others as reflections of our own tastes and values. So if you say most people have no inclination to imagine, to dream ... it is simply that you do not ... or that you have never given yourself a chance. After all, what is it that distinguishes us from what we call lower forms of life? It is the MIND that vast blank artist is a tablet waiting for the impressions of experience, of the lights and shadows on artichokes. The MIND—which can absorb, create and imagine."

1975 was to be the last year of the orderly, predictable graduations at Bexley. One might have expected a few fireworks for 1976–some red, white and blue confetti. Alas, Dr. Norman Samuels, the new principal, (certainly no artichoke watcher) saw no merit in fireworks, bicentennial otherwise. The very next year Dr. Samuels decreed there would be a shorter ceremony. Still four speakers–a faculty chosen speaker, a student selected speaker and the Valedictorian and Salutatorian finally to be identified. (Bexley was the last area school to give public recognition to its top academic students: a former Superintendent had thought such academic recognition too elitist). The Salutatorian would now give a short welcoming speech of the evening; the Valedictorian, a brief closing speech.

Administrative personnel never expected valedictorians and salutatorians to give dynamic speeches. Sometimes a faculty or board member would even say to me after the ceremony, wasn't the Student Speaker just SUPER?!?" I would smile my thanks. But I was thinking: on the logo of this school district is a lamp of learning, and beneath the lamp is the word "Excellence", and no, I don't think it's super for a speaker to spend our time telling a few warmed over jokes from TV-land. Have you noticed? The Student Speaker is never a girl, always a GUY Student Speaker.

Jerry Spence was just such a speaker, of the late 70's. During our preparation weeks (there were always about seventeen sessions of preparation), Jerry did not bother to show up for the first four meetings. I sent a report to the Assistant Principal and two days later received this note from Jerry himself.

Dear Mrs. Juditz,

    I spoke with Mr. Martin today
in respect to your concern about my
willingness to cooperate or even to make
a speech. I assure you that I fully intend
to make a speech, the best one of all if
possible. "Welfare of one means welfare of
all" will be related to my theme, although
it is not easy to work with and although
Mr. Wilkie was a loser. *My rough draft is
not complete because of a few problems in
relating the theme to what I want to say,
but I'm certain it will be complete
shortly, and when it is, I will be more
than happy to discuss it. Please DON'T
RUSH ME. It's hard enough, and please
trust me not to screw it up. My speech
will work fine and I'm sure will correlate
quite well with the others. As I have no
speech to practice and a 3:30 job interview I will go home to work on MY SPEECH.
You may think I'm a real punk smart-ass
but I'm really not ... Please understand.
I have to be left alone to think and
write. It will be good.

        Jeremiah M. Spence

* Is this really true?

By Session Ten, Jerry did have down on grubby paper a speech of sorts. From various student comments and the glazed look often in Jerry's eyes, I surmised that Jere was usually high by rehearsal time of day.

Speakers were expected to memorize speeches, yet they were allowed to have their script on the lectern_in case of a sudden bee sting, a dog jumping over the chain link fence, a parent taking a barrage of flash bulb shots, a helicopter flying directly over the field (hovering a bit to see what was really going on down there). Many were the out-door hazards that could break concentration.

Well, Jeremiah started out from the Cafeteria where the class procession began. He had that glazed look again, his tie was somewhat askew, though it was an appropriate tie. And he was wearing a real shirt and pressed trousers, real shoes and sox, along with his gown and mortarboard.

I said, "Good luck, Jerry. Remember, keep the volume up. Don't rush!"

"Mrs. J..."

"What, Jerry?"

"Mrs. J... I don't know where my speech is. I had a copy ... middle of the afternoon..."

"Oh, not to worry, Jerry. The speech will be right there on the lectern, when it's your turn."

Just fifteen minutes before this conversation I had anchored extra copies of all the speeches onto the lectern; the papers were weighted down with an iron brace, in case of a sudden breeze.

We all started to process. About forty minutes later

when it was Jerry's turn, he rose, walked to the lectern, looked down at the wooden slate. Still no words. Then, he looked across to where I was sitting.

Suddenly I knew what had happened. The Superintendent, who had spoken just before Jerry's turn, as a final dramatic gesture to his conclusion, had scooped up the two remaining scripts, saluting the audience with the papers as he left the lectern.

Oh, not to worry. On my lap I had the third back up copy for both remaining speakers. I rose carefully, walked calmly to the lectern and put the two scripts in place.

I have no memory of what Jeremiah Spence said. He was somewhat luckier than a speaker of another June evening, who was halfway through his speech when a sudden gust of wind sent the script flying in four directions. I moved in fast with my third back up script, but the speaker was at a loss to remember where he had been cut off.

By no means were all Student Speakers "glazed over". Some were very responsible leaders, or at least perceived as such. Still, there could be a crisis. As in the case of Roger.

Three days before graduation, Roger developed chicken pox a full-blown case of chicken pox. He was covered, literally covered, with pink, itchy blotches. But Roger was determined to speak: he was Student Council President, he had been a contestant in State speech tournaments, he had worked long hours on his graduation speech. Roger was determined to speak. The other speakers had all had chicken pox, so had I in 1938. We had nothing to fear from Roger.

Not so Mr. Harvey, the school Principal, who feared if word got about as to Roger's condition, the administration, the school nurse, the township Board of Health, or somebody, would consider it an act of extreme negligence in the interest of all persons present to allow Roger to participate in the graduation ceremonies. Mr. Harvey, also recalling how determined Roger could be in all his Student Council activities, wisely decided to effect a compromise.

Since the ceremonies were to be held outdoors, in the fresh air of the stadium, Roger would be allowed to participate if he entered the stadium alone, walking about 15 paces behind the other graduates, and were to sit off by himself, fifteen to twenty feet from any other participants. He would have his own script with him at all times, and not touch the lectern nor anybody else. He would rise when his name was called at the time of awarding diplomas, but he would not come forward to receive the (fake) diploma.

Come to think of it, Roger was not to be the first graduating Senior who was not allowed to accept his fake diploma. Several years before, there had been Peter Lakelski, who refused to wear a necktie and sox as part of his graduation outfit. Peter's father had accosted Mr. Harvey just before the ceremony and threatened to smash in his nose, but the stadium custodian had intervened by swinging shut the entrance gate, leaving Mr. Lakelski outside and Mr. Harvey in line with the approaching procession. There had also been the twenty-nine boys with hair longer than regulation length in the '70's, including Hank

Nace, who won his "fifteen minutes of fame" in the community became of his newspaper interview about the subject.

But to finish the story about Roger's graduation... The following year, when we were again driven indoors by bad weather, Mr. Harvey was pelted with marshmallows from some of the class members as he began his introductory remarks to the diploma sequence of the program. The missiles came from somewhere in the back rows of all those Seniors seated behind him, I never thought this through before, but as I write about that evening I suddenly remember: Roger's brother was graduating. Just possibly, could it have been Edward who started the bombardment? Roger must have been in the audience, just as possibly enjoying his vindication for his graduation speech in the "great alone".

About 25 years ago, an article appeared in a national educational journal: the title of the piece was "Are Commencements Obsolete?" A survey had been conducted and two significant facts emerged: parents and students in large numbers favored the continuation of the commencement ceremony; large numbers of parents and students believed the commencement program should be formulated by students and administration with approval granted by the school board.

About 25 years before that survey was conducted, I had graduated from the central high school of a small eastern city. The 817 graduating class members presented a pageant which a committee of ten seniors, guided by the Latin teacher, had written. I served on that committee; we worked all winter on the script. Perhaps it took us such a long time because we were the first graduating class to experience the impact of the atomic bomb on civilization. Graduating classes before us had to deal with such topics as, Who Is the Educated Man? As Citizens, What Should Our Values be? Or The Real Meaning of Freedom.

By comparison, our theme seemed like a sick joke: How do you survive in a world with Atomic Weapons? After weeks of discussion, we decided to liken the atom bomb to Prometheus bringing fire to Man. My own era of crisis and chaos was the Industrial Revolution. There were guidelines for the pageant. Every class member was to play three different characters, have three different costumes; the musicians, actors, singers, dancers who had shown exceptional talent in their high school career, would have featured roles. All of this had to fit within a three-hour time frame. As to the budget, there was no mention. Costumes were always rented from an old, reliable Philadelphia firm. The Latin teacher and I traveled by train and spent an entire day in Philadelphia reserving the costumes, reviewing the size charts and accessory colors for 817 people. Times three equals 2451. Costuming our high school graduation was as good as doing two years' worth of full cast Broadway shows!

How did we come by such an elaborate graduation, long before the day of surveys? Our Drama Director was one of the founders of the International Thespian Society. He was a workaholic, a fire-and-brimstone director, a dynamic fund raiser (and a very ordinary English teacher). I feared him. I would have walked barefoot on nails on a dirty stage at his direction. He cast me as Lorraine Sheldon in "The Man Who Came to Dinner". Overnight I was famous at School.

The graduation program at Bexley was more like a standard college commencement, except that our only near-famous speaker was a state senator, that same math teacher who had left early, on the day of the TMI accident and gone into politics. A handful of students over the years had chosen NOT to participate in the ceremony, but despite all the upheaval at schools in the latter decades of the 20th century—in university, college, high school, even on down to the kindergarten level—I have not heard of any school that has done away with the graduation program". I suspect that the feeling about this tradition is best understood by an incident I experienced right after a Bexley graduation.

I was heading to the parking lot set against a green hill next to the school tennis courts. The June evening was mild, the sunset a narrow band of coral against the pale blue sky. Standing at the top of the low green hill was my neighbor, Kimberly Wentz, still in her graduation gown. Kimberly lived across the street from me. During most of her school career she had worn black only, long before the time of the Gothic trend of the 90's. Suddenly, Kimberly lifted her arm and waved. Then, in her sparkling white gown and mortarboard and matching pumps, she dropped to her knees and began rolling down the hill, laughing and shouting, tumbling over and over.

Graduation from school is the celebration of freedom, and the invitation to follow your dreams.

"Dare to err and dream-deep
meaning often lies in
childish plays."

-Schiller

Who's In Charge Here?

By 1995 Dr. Gary Ellis, Superintendent of the Shore School District, had served twenty-five years in administrative posts, and was now paid $110,688. If any reader is in doubt about what a Superintendent is, does, expects to do, this admin bulletin will help clarify the responsibility of Dr. Ellis.

"Your school board is composed of nine members, three elected from each of the three regions which make up the South Shore School District. Although board members (also known as directors) are elected by voters in each of these regions, each represents the entire district. Directors are elected to serve four-year terms of office. The Superintendent of Schools serves as an ex officio member of the Board. He sits with the Board as an advisor, but he does not vote. It is the responsibility of the Board to establish policy for the operation of the schools and the education of all persons from five to twenty-one years of age living in the South Shore district. The Board bears the responsibility for levying and collecting taxes and approving expenditures for the operation of the schools. The Board is responsible for approving the appointment of all personnel who work in the District and for setting the scope and direction of the program of instruction."

In one short sentence, the taxpayer should be running the show, via-the Board.

Gary did not see the power structure in the same light. And he had his loyal followers. One board member gushed, "I have no trouble justifying his salary. He is an extraordinary worker, unbelievably well-organized. We board members agree all information is at our fingertips all of the time.

That bedazzled board member did not know how scrupulously Dr. Ellis kept all his flock in line, how the next five years would create a plot that even our newspaper (not known for its crusading nature) would assign special reporters to cover, and run a hardly flattering photo of the South Shore Super well over twenty times. In the photo, the eyes were squinting a bit, the mouth pursed. The jowly cheeks combined to make him look contemptuous of the scene he was surveying.

But to start at the beginning: Dr. Ellis was hired in 1983 at a salary of $50,000. His predecessor had been paid to leave early after he lost an anti-defamation suit by principal Dr. Nathan Samuels. That's an interesting story, too, but suffice to say, the super of that era was anti-Jewish, said so, and Dr. Samuels took exception, recourse and won his suit.

When Gary Ellis applied for the position, there were 112 highly qualified candidates. Maybe. I'm not sure who was giving leaks about the count." If there really were 112 conten-ders, only one had the contact(s) needed to gain the position. That was Gary. A further leak informed that Gary had to-leave his last position, where he'd had an unfortunate encounter with the teachers union: conversations of union members allegedly had been wire tapped by a close assistant of Gary. The final negotiation at the bargaining table was: Dr. Ellis if you leave, we'll agree to the offer.

And Gary left, to warmer, safer waters and surely a close friend or two at South Shore.

By the time South Shore teachers struck in 1988, Gary had a full circle of really close friends, and his wife

Faye, a realtor, was friendly to all of us, greeted us by name, with a smile, always. At the time of the Strike, the Board President, the Board Vice President, the insurance agent (a board member) whose office was directly across the street from Bexley High, and a brother-in-law of Gary (not on the Board but brought in to fill a newly created administrative position)–these were five bosom buddies.

As Gary himself once said (to his assigned news reporter), "I'm running a 58 million dollar enterprise, that's what I'm really doing."

Gary was actually saying, I'm worth every penny they pay me. (About $87,500 at that point.) No hint that he should be working for the Board elected by taxpayers of South Shore. He seemed to feel that he owned us as a business: He was the CEO. Power seems to beget power, and in the next three years Gary moved to less low-profile activities. While teacher transfers, still a residual from the '88 strike, edged upward, and new administrative posts were created, a newer, much larger administrative building emerged from the renovation of a former electronics factory, which we all assumed had been sold through Mrs. Ellis' firm. Certainly no sidewalk marchers of any future strikes could walk in front of this admin building: it was set in a hillside down from an expressway, a strong chain link fence wound round the entire complex. There was an official autho-rized entrance, which was occasionally confused with the entrance to the Regional Police grounds immediately next door.

Now about Gary's new activities', as reported by our local paper. The first incident had to do directly with Gary's assistant, Dr. Emma Fenton, in charge of arranging retirement earnings. A teacher/coach who had to take early retirement because of ill health appeared at Emma's office in late summer.

At that interview Emma said he'd have to pay back $25,000 in sabbatical earnings if he did not fulfill a one-year-post sabbatical teaching obligation. Against the advice of his cardiologist, the teacher agreed to fulfill the teaching obligation. Later that day Emma called him back to say this obligation did not apply in a case of medical reasons. Two days later Emma discussed with him his retirement bonus payments–$9,000. This was NOT approved by the Board; the teacher/coach appealed, saying he had been intentionally deceived. At the arbitration hearing, Dr. Fenton said she had never said $9,000 would be awarded as bonus retirement earnings.

The President of the School Board backed up Emma and said caustically to the teacher (who had been employed for more then 30 years): "It is patently unfair for you to claim substantial benefit more than two months after the school board approved your retirement in a manner which forgave substantial teaching obligation on your part."

One board member did offer the opinion that the retirement earnings were being withheld on a technicality and that there had been poor communication in the entire process.

Superintendent Ellis said nothing at all. Had he already locked in the board vote to match Emma's decision? Had he made the decision for Emma? Did he simply not like the teacher/coach?

The teacher/coach never did get his $9,000 that Emma Fenton said he would: He lost his case and it was not clear how well the union had backed his appeal. I was explaining this case to a friend recently, and she asked, "How does the union get involved? I know that the Superintendent does not have a vote, although he may comment; the vote by the board is what counts. So how can the union make a difference?

"If an employee takes exception to a ruling by the Board, he/she may appeal to the union. In the case of the teacher/coach it was not clear how well the union had backed him. The union president now had some other worries and a case of her own. She had entered a grievance against the District when two letters from the admin staff criticizing the union and her leadership had shown up in her personnel file. The admin members said the letters were put in the wrong file."

"And then what was her replay?" asked my friend.

"OK, I'll withdraw the grievance when the District outlines the mistake in writing, one letter from Gary Ellis and one from Lester Rand."

(Lester, Director of Personnel, was a recent addition to Gary's circle of bosom buddies.)

The Union president politely explained the focus of her grievance: issues regarding her role as union President should not be in the file which center on professional development. Dr. Ellis' response was–"please send any questions by fax"; she did and received no answer. Lester Rand finally replied, "I strongly dispute any intimidation or mistreatment of teachers".

"Ohhh" was all my friend said. And then she added, "Was it beneath Dr. Ellis' dignity to answer a polite letter politely; was it outside his scope of administrative technique to teach a subordinate to answer a polite letter politely?"

Perhaps Dr. Ellis never sent any direct reply because he was now involved in a very high profile case, a federal trial involving the former District solicitor William Trone. Attorney Trone had been charged with over billing South Shore and ten other school districts for legal services. Ellis was one of four superintendents who allegedly authorized Trone to use a graduated scale outlining on his firm stationary to inflate bills for service. Trone was facing 11 counts of mail fraud, 5 counts obstruction of justice. From 1992 to 1993 he had over billed by $81,000. Yet South Shore reappointed his firm one month after the federal jury handed down an indictment.

The Board president, Edward Slade, claimed Trone innocent, said they could find no discrepancies: We stand by Trone! Let the jury determine! US attorney Myer Johnson said Trone inflated bills: "It was to recoup the cost of free work they did for admin members and school board members on personal legal matters. A former associate in Trone's firm discussed the inflated bills: "I was authorized by Ellis instead of raising the hourly rate from 75 to 85 dollars; Dr. Ellis said it was too politically risky."

Ellis was present at this trial; we never learned what his explanation was, but it was leaked that Personnel Director Lester Rand said," It is an allegation. That's all it is. The office Manager mistakenly inflated all bills."

To make a very long story very short, Solicitor Trone was sentenced to 33 months in prison. In private conversations, I understand that Gary still thinks Good Ole Bill is innocent.

A few months after testifying at the Trone trial, Gary had another challenge very close to home: A group of students tired of how its district officials play scrambled eggs with the faculty. Seventy-five very vocal Bexley students protested tentative transfers of two art teachers and a guidance counselor.

They staged a sit-in at the Bexley school lobby. (I told you it was next to impossible to gain admittance to the district office compound, and no one could see what was going on there anyway, unless you happened to glance down hurriedly from the big highway.)

The leader of the sit-in, Alec Simov, a fourth year, award winning art student "We have lost faith going through the proper channels–joining advisory committees, writing letter's filling out comment sheets."

And a great cheer went up from the other seventy-four students.

Few answers were forthcoming from the admins that day or the next. So, six students drove to the Admin Office. A custodian unlocked the chain link fence of the compound, and the students were allowed to meet with Lester Rand.

"I want you to know," Mr. Rand said, "that transfers are voluntary or strategic for educational benefit for students and teachers. Now I know the Union argues transfers are punitive and an intimidation tactic, reflexive of a bitter '89 strike." (He was wrong, it was an '88 strike.) Angeline Thomas spoke up.

"Mr. Rand, our teachers, Alice Benson and Catherine Richardson broke down in class when they learned they were on the transfer block and were to go to elementary school. Oh yes, they'll be paid the same to cut out pumpkins."

Alec Simov joined in.

"Mr. Rand, our teachers have worked years building an award winning program. This is scary, and it makes us very angry. We don't know if it's because someone spoke out at some point or what."

Sheila Dennis had a question about the counselor's transfer.

"Why should these people leave when we're so attached to them now? It's so hard to build a trust in some-one else."

Mr. Rand had no comments; he thanked them for coming down to the headquarters. They left the building and the custodian unlocked the big gate to let them pass through. The next several weeks brought forth no answers, no explanations, no follow-up letter from Gary Ellis. In fact no one would ever know what Gary looked or sounded like, except for the smirking portrait that had appeared many times in the local paper, and the halting, unenthusiastic reading of his commencement welcoming speech.

At this point there was an update in Gary's tangle with Bill Trone: Trone was serving his prison sentence; the auditor general of the state was gathering information on which school districts were to get what monies back. Originally the South Shore Board President had estimated about $1300 was South Shore's share. As things finally turned out, South Shore received $6,610.00. Gary and Bill were perhaps better buddies then Bill and other supers: Bill was ordered to pay back a total of $60,000 to 45 over billed schools. Ten percent went to one district–South Shore. I've often wondered, when the money came back, did it go to the Library for books more recent then '76? To the auditorium for recovering badly damaged upholstery? To the hall roof, where rain seeped in on bad days?

By Springtime 1997, Gary Ellis was hard at work on his new contract, and his roving reporter for the paper wrote," School's chief averse to any open Board criticism... a freedom of expression clause in Ellis' contract has been called highly unusual by some state academic officials and raising questions within the district. Does the clause tilt balance of power, curb discussion on important issues, or merely give Gary Ellis more confidence to do his job? The clause is as follows: The superintendent and the school board recognize that the public interest is not served by public criticism of performance of either party. This has led the State Association of Administrators to ask, 'Why does the Board protect Ellis from itself-who's in charge here?'

I asked my neighbor, Marian Clark, "What is it really that glues this pack together? Any one of the things that have been happening could be enough to get Gary Ellis out of here?"

"I'm not really sure", she replied. "My suspicion is

that it has to do with real estate...certain people holding on to very desirable tracts.

"You mean something large enough for sub-division?"

Marion had been in real estate herself awhile back, and had been surprised at times to learn who in the District owned what property.

"Whatever it is," I said, "it has to do with money, a large amount of holdings–property or stock in certain companies. Remember, the Board has 80 million to spend on anything from land contracts to band uniforms..."

The argument about the freedom of expression clause went on in the local paper. Finally, the reporter received a statement from the board President, Edward Slade. "You shouldn't hang your dirty laundry out!" (Slade was never accused of being erudite). Ellis made a statement, too: "The language is clear and unambiguous. It's intended to promote a harmonious relationship between and among board members and the Superintendent."

There was another statement, this time from an ex-director of the State School Boards, and doubtless prefaced with a hearty belly laugh: "That's not a clause you need to start a trusting relationship. The Superintendent has to understand he works for the Board."

As it turned out, this clause was laying the groundwork for Gary's forthcoming ventures: violation of the States Sunshine Act, issues of nepotism and federal suit by six South Shore teachers against the district, for transfer related to gender and age.

Our state's Sunshine Law requires that the boards of public agencies meet in public with certain specific exceptions. A violation may be punished by a fine of up to $100. The "slap on the wrist punishment for violation would lead one to believe that this law does not seem to command respect. In all of Gary's manipulations, however, this is the one that drew blood from the city editor of the paper, resulting in a half-page message, "CONTRACT WITH PUBLIC BROKEN".

To scrutinize what Dr. Ellis had done: contract time was about to take place for Gary and his two assistants, Emma Fenton and Lester Rand. The meeting where the vote was to be taken was open to the public, but on that November evening no contract item appeared on the agenda. Nor did any one of the eight school board members present even mention that this was a 1.5 million five-year salary package under consideration. Instead, these three contracts were handled in a single blanket motion that covered 75 individual employees, including custodians, cafeteria workers and bus drivers, a motion that was approved without discussion or debate. If only for PR points, if only because Gary was always eager to point out that he was running the state's most complex educational enterprise, should not Ellis and Company have extended to citizens and taxpayers of the South Shore District the chance to ask questions about the "3-contract 1.5 million deal" and offer their comments? Why did the school board go out of its way to keep the contract renewal out of public view?

Perhaps timing had something to do with it, perhaps the Board sensed that the Sunshine Law was not uppermost in the minds of the Union members: the "N" word had risen to the top of SSEA'S list of concerns–NEPOTISM. It was not really a household word with all families in the district (occasionally I had to translate in conversation). Nepotism–the hiring of admin and school board members' relatives. This practice was not allowed between 1977 and '93, when the policy had been changed. The Union was saying–"nepotism's fringe benefits, subtle, blatant or perceived–have demoralized many teachers." A statistician had reported: at least 25 percent of all South Shore employees are related to another employee.

Comments by the Union President were more specific. There are the haves and the have-nots. A teacher with a tech-nology degree being passed over for a computer job because she was basically told that she didn't associate with the right people. We might not resent the nepotism policy if there were not evidence of favoritism. I mean I don't think this would be a problem if we worked for an administration that was friendly, people-oriented and cooperative."

I suddenly remembered the comment of a letter-to-the editor writer–"This district is not family friendly!" Well, it depends which families you're talking about.

Nepotism was a number one concern of the union for seven years, but that long road had a sharp turning as the new millennium began: the policy was reversed. To a degree. A 5-3 Board vote "forbids the hiring of immediate family, aunts, uncles, first cousins or in-laws of school board members, the Superintendent, and the Assistant Superintendents. It does not apply to principals and other management employees, part timers, day to day subs or extra duty employees, such as coaches.

With the new policy in place, transfer issues were brought from the back burner–six teachers with a combined 100 years of teaching experience in South Shore District charged the district with age and sex discrimination. Charges were filed with the State Human Relations Commission by SSEA lawyers on behalf of the six. There was a common theme, a continuing pattern and practice of involuntary transfers that discriminate against women and teachers over 40 South Shore Education Association had tried to convince the District these transfers were unsettling for staff and students, that they destroy the concept of neighborhood schools, frustrate parent/teacher relationships and contribute to intimidation.

Of the six teachers, there was just one I had known personally and admired immensely–Amy Martindale, home economics. Teacher for 24 years at Bexley. She had instituted the parenting program in the late '80's: tiny tots from a number of district families would participate in a six-weeks program to teach the teen-age surrogate moms the behavioral skills to cope with the "terrible two's, and there were valuable extra lessons in nutrition, sewing and mending hygiene. Amy was the teacher who in the Strike of '88 brought us the delicious fixings for lunch on the picket line. Always so encouraging, always positive ... Amy was now to be transferred??? To a Middle School!!! Her strength was in high school issues!!!!!!!

Dr. Ellis called the complaints puzzling—"all transfers are centered on the needs of students". One of Gary's newest assistants, when asked by the roving reporter how many transfers were given in the current season, the assistant, Ralph Lentz, refused to give the number. And he added, "It's our prerogative how we fuel you". One thing especially about close contact with Gary—his arrogance rubbed off. I remember when Ralph was a PRINCIPAL at Bexley: he had always been very civil, helpful even to staff members—qualities not all principals sought to emulate. In the same week that brought these puzzling moments to Gary, there was a board meeting, described by the paper's reporter as a "tumultuous meeting".

In the reporter's own words, "during a meeting marked by a high level resignation and demands from spectators", Edward Slade, the Board President, was nominated to serve another two-year term. It was a dead locked ballot: no 9th board member was there to vote the swing vote. Ed was finally replaced (temporarily) by a former athletic director. Then, from the audience, the township commissioner, Roberta Stewart, demanded the three Admin salaries that had been railroaded through at the previous board meeting be declared null and void.

Mrs. Stewart stated further that she would form a citizens' action committee. Lester Rand then announced his retirement (a real surprise), which decision he said had nothing to do with all of the problems at hand. (He was right about that-his decision had to do with his son, who until recently had been serving as a solicitor for the board when it was discovered he had vested interests in a health plan he was promoting for teachers.) Dr. Ellis told Lester he would be sorely missed, then Gary distributed pages–of statistics about the local paper's negative reports, where-upon the newest board member, Martin Blair, a former student of mine, rose and said, "Well, Dr. Ellis, they got the story straight, didn't they?" It is not recorded what comment Gary made at this point in the tumultuous meeting. I recalled how well Martin, in speech class years. before, had always contributed to the daily news discussions.

And, I recalled how difficult had been Martin's struggle to get elected to the board the year before. Months before election time, Martin had made a study of his neighborhood elementary school which the board wished to replace instead of renovate. He gathered all the comparative data on replacement vs. renovation, he printed this information land distributed it to 11 residents in the area. He took an opinion survey of all these people and brought his findings to the board.

I remember that board meeting, held on a mid-March evening–chill indoors and out. I arrived a half hour early and managed to get a seat. Very few board meetings had this kind of attendance. Many items were on the agenda, but Martin Blair's survey and the resulting newspaper articles had brought most of the crowd. As the board entered, one member took a quick look and his eyebrows shot up. Gary Ellis entered last and took his seat to the right of the president, Edward Slade. Then we all had to scramble to our feet to pledge allegiance to the flag.

On the printed agenda were items ranging from recognition of Youth Art Month billboard artists to athletic training equipment and supplies for fall sports, the only hint of Martin's survey and report was listed as "PlanCon sub-mittals Hillcrest Jefferson Heights–the next step in the process of planning for the replacement of these two ele-mentary schools. There was still standing room. Only the hour was half-past nine. (We had pledged the flag at 7:30).

When finally it was Martin's turn to speak (all per-sons planning to speak had had to apply for a special per-mission card), the first question Dr. Ellis asked him was, "What is your profession?"

Martin, 6'5", lanky as in high school days, adjusted his spectacles and replied, "I am a kitchen contractor".

Superintendent Ellis curled his bottom lip, as he always did when he wanted to look smirky. Martin began his report, explained his survey results to date showed double for renovation against replacement and that a neighbor-hood school was preferred to a large area elementary school. Martin's complete plan included reopening a former small neighborhood school in the area southeast of Hillcrest.

There was debate for and against Martin's proposal. Finally, a tall, silver haired lady rose and said, "Thank you Mr. Blair, for what you have done. You prove to us that final-ly someone is interested in local government." There was a round of strong applause.

Preservationist that I am, I did not personally believe the existing Hillcrest was an architectural treasure–from the outside it was one-story, unpretentious, rather drab. But once inside the building, you noticed that each series of rooms was designed around a courtyard (where ducks quite often raised their families). There was a fine stage for concerts and plays. There was a pleasant cafeteria—even on overcast days there was plenty of natural lighting. I understood what Martin meant about a neighborhood school; it was the size school where all the teachers, all the boys and girls would know each other. My own daughter had had very happy years at Hillcrest...

Martin's mission to renovate Hillcrest did not succeed, but his hard work and his determination to point the school board in a direction that would give citizens some insight into how to make their schools more effective did have impact. He won his bid for board election, had the support of three other board members. Especially he had the courage to open debate on issues at board meetings.

To focus again on the tumultuous meeting a year after Martin presented his proposal—all that dirty laundry (as Ed Slade had said) was flapping out there in the sunshine, harder to endure because he didn't get reelected as board President.

Before the next board meeting right after Christmas, Dr. Emma Fenton revealed to a reporter that she, as the mother of a student, found the idea of a Citizens' Committee very frightening. At the same meeting, the Principal at Bexley, (not the blackmailing one from my era, but one just as unethical) stated to the reporter, "All we have heard about is fabrication, half-truths and incomplete information in the paper". Martin Blair asked the Principal, "Don't you have any respect for the democratic process?"

Next day, Emma sent round a directive to all teachers and principals, urging them to be very careful about their selection of newspaper for class assignments. Any orders for newspapers would have to go through her office.

To answer Martin Blair's question about the democratic process: No, these persons do not have any respect for the democratic process, nor for their colleagues, nor the families who have entrusted their children to these schools. The best evidence I have for believing this is GARY'S GAZETTE.

A few months before, at the time of the November elections when Martin Blair was running his campaign to elect enough new board members to tip the scales against Gary's high-handed dealings, a board member who had recently resigned mentioned to me, "You know, before I was on the board, I had never even heard of Gary's newsletter..."

"Newsletter? What newsletter?" I asked.

"The one he gives to each board member before a meeting... he calls it Gary's Gazette", and the man chuckled.

"What's in the newsletter?"

Oh, quite a lot really. Information on education, District initiatives, and Ellis' personal opinions. You might see anything from construction project updates and student disciplinary matters to sport team results and media articles on education".

"I gather much of this is written with a personal touch?" "Oh yes—one item about a construction project referred to a borough Planning Commission member as having "harebrained" ideas. In one headline, "So Who's the Bozo"–he referred to an elementary school teacher as gossipy". He uses the newsletter as an editorial platform..."

"And you started receiving this as soon as you were on the Board. What was your reaction?" I asked. "I felt uncomfortable with some of the content. I think a lot of times what made me uncomfortable was that through his editorializing, and a lot of times through his satirizing, he was trying to form board opinion on issues. HE was telling us how to vote. And I guess the most unsettling thing was the way he delivered the Gazette to us..."

"You mean he hand delivered this to each of you, all nine of you?"

"Often Ellis brought it around. Sometimes Ralph Lentz delivered it. Generally, it was late at night, either when I was putting the kids to bed or just after. The car would come up the driveway, I'd hear it, and then it would leave. I'd go out and there would be my manila envelope leaning against the door with Gary's Gazette in it."

Then that was how each board member knew what was expected of him/her, how to vote without any risky debate, which motion would include what contract(s). No wonder years ago that one board member had said so enthusiastically, "Dr. Ellis is unbelievably well-organized. We board members have all information at our fingertips all of the time,"

Readers will have some more questions–how many people joined the Citizens' Action Committee? Aside from the nepotism policy, was nothing ever turned around, from January 1999 to January 2001? How come this super wasn't bought out, the way the anti-Semitic one was?

There were regularly from 40 to 70 persons who attended the Citizens committee. Two new elementary schools were built against the wishes of the majority of parents. Seventeen percent of all teachers continued to be transferred–the federal case of THE SIX has yet to be resolved. A web site on the Internet appeared with vitriolic remarks about some former teachers of the district.

A new picture of Dr. Ellis began appearing with the articles in the paper. This Dr. Ellis was about 40 pounds heavier, his toupee now matched better the gray sideburns. He is sitting in a high-backed chair; the lips are still pursed, but the eyes hold no trace of a smile–they hold all the friendliness of a chain link fence.

This picture first appeared when the newer board had called for his ouster. His reply was, "Members of the public and new board members cannot fully appreciate the complexity of running a school district until they have actually been serving as directors for a time. He added that the new members were hasty when calling for his ouster.

These comments brought a trickle of letters-to-the-editor, but it was not until a few months later that a new hornets' nest of public opinion was uncovered: it became known as "Lasergate".

A group of middle school students had gone on an end-of-school trip with parents and teacher chaperones to Washington DC. During the day, the students had a chance to buy some souvenirs; some had chosen small laser beam key chains. In fact, one of the parent chaperones had said these key chains would be a great memento of the trip. None of the adults in the group remembered about a brief addition to the weapons' policy within the past year. You'll remember in the earlier chapter about weapons most everything in school was regarded as a weapon. Lasers were added to the list. Of course, when the original policy was put into effect, laser fun things had not yet been invented.

Anyway, when the 17 middle schoolers, the teachers and parent chaperones all returned from the nation's capitol, they discovered they were in deep trouble. The Administration let it be known that when school reopened in the autumn there would be PUNISHMENT: probation, in-school suspension, community service and the writing of a 500-word essay. The parent chaperones were not pleased. They requested a conference with Dr. Gary Ellis. They were ignored. They wrote letters-to-the-editor of the paper. These were not ignored at all. They called for an ouster of Gary; the new Gary picture was run with the article. But no real progress was made until autumn. A few days before school began, the President of the school board, Rebecca Charles, finally did call a conference, with Gary seated at the table, too. She announced that all proposed punishment on the laser key chain incident had been rescinded.

A great cheer went up from the assembled parents and students and other board members. Only Dr. Ellis remained silent, solidly stolid. Next day, all of the parents involved sent a letter to Commissioner Stewart, alerting her to their interest in joining the Citizens Action Committee.

The parent chaperones joined the Citizens' Action Committee; South Shore School District Weapons' Policy now has an addendum: "Weapon is defined by object's use". Translated–a key chain is not a weapon.

A reader's last question: will the district finally get rid of Gary? Ironically, of all the things that could have brought him down–his support for a convicted felon, his violation of the state's Sunshine law, his demeaning policy of transfers for teachers–it was the "little laser Key chain" that brought forth the wrath of parents. As of this writing, Spring 2001, the Board has two more months to decide whether or not to put Gary's contract renewal on a regular meeting agenda, allow for debate and take a vote. Already the board has been cautioned by the new solicitor to be wary about debating Gary's past performance because of the unique clause in his contract. What do I think will happen?

At the time of the last election for new school board members, an interesting article appeared in our local paper. Roughly translated, the writer said that one in five persons in the county would turn out at the polls. At stake was 186 million dollars of taxpayer money to finance eight county school districts in the coming year. So why the poor turnout?

First of all, the taxpayer feels that the schools are run well. The taxpayer doesn't know much about government, less about local government. It's a mix of alienation, lack of information and the perception that local government doesn't matter much in his/her life. The global fuss about education does not translate into voter interest in school boards.

That taxpayer doesn't know the power and authority at the local school board level. He's never met Gary, doesn't know anything about Gary's Gazette. And I can add, even if he takes the daily paper (with all its recent articles about the super, complete with the super's photos), he mostly reads the sports section the obits possibly, glances at the cartoons and a few ads under "automotive", then throws the paper in the recycle bin.

What will happen in June? There is a hint that Gary is almost as unsure about the outcome as many of us are: he has said he is thinking of retirement. That's partly because at least two of the board members let it be known that unlike the anti-defamation case, Ellis would be too costly to buy out. That's also partly because winning a new contract is not a sure thing: the Board is as close as a split down the center; with one member absent, there will be no one to break the tie. The contract length is open to three, four or five years–perhaps Gary is wondering how soon would all this be coming to a head once more? Three of his closest relatives are district employees; with the new nepotism policy, no other relatives will be hired.

In a very recent interview, Dr. Ellis was also pointing out how his position consumed at least 70 hours a week–the usual business hours, the evening meetings, the sports events. Well, be that as it may, in all his years at South Shore he was never seen-to attend a speech nor drama competition, and we were often a regional host school. When we received the School of the Year award, presented by the State Speech Association for our complete speech and theatre program, I never received any note or call of congratulations from his office. Perhaps we did appear in Gary's Gazette; if we did, we'll never know, will we?

There is a Dutch proverb that ought to be remembered by who's-in-charge-here—it will serve perhaps as an encouraging thought about Gary's future contract:

```
"Who wants the last drop out
of the can gets the lid on
his nose."
```

The Great Pumpkin Travels

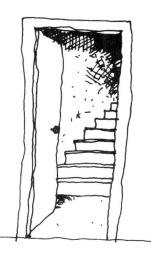

Another series of happenings that Dr. Gary Ellis never included in his seventy-hour working week was Bexley Hills Children's Theatre. Perhaps we did have a mention in Gary's Gazette.

From early Spring, all the way to Memorial Day, we performed plays at the District elementary schools. At least eight of the fifteen schools, with two different casts. There were those Bexley teachers (especially social studies teachers who taught from. the same lecture material, on the same date, year after year) who did not cotton to having a student out of class, ever. Thus, there were two casts, each with its own costumes and hand props. Large props could be used by both casts, a large prop such as the machine for "The Invention". The machine had multiple parts, easily assembled and taken apart... (the machine produced CANDIES).

South Shore's elementary schools were scattered about, rather like the naturalizing of daffodils (an experienced gardener distributing the bulbs) a few clustered, others closely related, and the final two of the total fifteen were flung far into another county. When I was first hired at Bexley, Mrs. Grant whom I was replacing said, "I always wanted a children's theatre program. If you continue this one on a permanent basis, never give it up. It's much harder to get something back once you've let it go.

I considered that philosophy very sound, and I applied it many times—to personal property (my stop watches), school curriculum (Speech compulsory for graduation), even my extra desk in the Teacher's Furnace Room Lounge. I WOULD KEEP IT ALL TOGETHER, I promised the departing Mrs. Grant.

One Springtime we did a new release of "Cinderella". That season, the son of the head of the Social Studies Department was playing the role of the Prince, and his other assignment was props coordinator. Walt was exceptionally enthusiastic the day he brought in the pumpkin.

"Mrs. J, look what I found at my uncle's farm!"

"Walt, that is positively the biggest most beautiful pumpkin I've ever seen...

"You'll never guess its weight... EIGHTY POUNDS!!"

The 80-pound prize pumpkin was already in my room when I had arrived that morning. I was curious as to how Walt had landed it.

"Oh, Jeff gave me a hand..." (Jeff was the Student Director) and you realize, it's just the weight of a kid. A lot of little kids don't weigh more than about 80 pounds."

I did not wish to put a damper on his pumpkin plans, but the logistics of hauling the Great One onto the bus off the bus, into the day's elementary school stage, back again to the bus, off the bus, back to Bexley, out of the bus, into my classroom...for EIGHT WEEKS???????!!!!!!

A rabbi had once said, "Youth is not a time of life, it is a state of mind. Youth means a temperamental predominance of courage over timidity, of the appetite for adventure over a life of ease."

Well, we would see how all the travels would turn out. Meanwhile, I was mentally reviewing our stages for the season. Stages at elementary schools are in multi-purpose rooms: the place where there is often a cafeteria, where students taking music lessons meet the teacher of instrumental instruction, where there is gym class twice a week, where art shows are hung, where remedial reading class is scheduled, where children's theatre plays are performed.

The stage, if you're lucky, is centered in the space on the wall opposite the cafeteria kitchen. We often performed where this was not the case: the stage was one-third of the room off center. I've never come across a name for this kind of playing space—not proscenium arch, nor theatre in the round, nor three-sided theatre. Maybe QUARTER ROUND?

Since these were multi-purpose rooms, the teachers in charge assumed the stage was a multi-storage space: music stands, cellos, portable blackboards, a battered desk, folding chairs, gym mats were all stored on the stage, and sometimes the more unusual—a deep freezer filled with Popsicles. I learned about the contents of the freezer only after I noticed several cast members munching (without permission) on Popsicles.

There were, among the stages, some very fine acting spaces. We looked forward to playing on these, for a time. One of the best, at the school farthest to the south in the district, was exceptional. Dimensions ideal, a lighting panel—WORKING, clean velvet curtains, also WORKING. There was an entrance, right and left stage, a back wall free of fire drill instruction. No music paraphernalia.

I should have known—it was all too good to last. Our van arrived at New Creek School on a cloud-free spring day. As we pulled up, the Principal of the school, Myrtle Baker, was waiting to greet us.

"Hello there, Mrs. Juditz!" I put the van in temporary

park.

"Isn't it a gorgeous day?" I said. Myrtle seemed to hesitate a moment, then she said,

I'm not sure anyone has told you, we made a computer room out of the stage." She chuckled. My smile was still glued to my face.

"Oh well, let me have a look." I looked with utter dismay. They had added a fourth wall where the velvet curtain had been. Aside from all the computer gear in the acting space, they had added a SOLID WALL. It did, however, have a door. The space left to us was three feet deep, eighteen feet wide; there were some steps down on either side to the main floor, No curtain, no lights...

"Oh, we'll adjust", I told Myrtle, " We'll make good use of those side steps."

I told the cast how and when to enter (after the audience would be in place, how to adjust blocking, how to learn balance quickly and not topple off the "stage". I refrained from telling Myrtle that I thought an unconscionable act had been committed against her school, that she must be very distressed.

On second thought, I doubted that Myrtle cared one way or the other. Did Myrtle really know what she had lost? I had always thought of the computer as a new type of "filing cabinet"–a tool to store a bulk of information. You could play games with it, unlike the tinny four-drawer file case. But still, it was the computer, a "file cabinet."

And with just a chuckle, Myrtle had traded a stage for a filing cabinet????!!!!. Still, she was not alone in her limited understanding of what a space for children's theatre really meant.

Bexley Children's Theatre occasionally had invitations to perform at specific community events: the Spring Arts Festival, held outdoors in the Bexley Courtyard; private schools, such as North Shore Montessori School; the Book Sale, sponsored by the South Shore Public Library–this performance was held in a mall, next to a playful fountain; and one season we were invited to appear at-the largest downtown hotel for a workshop session of the State Speech Association.

The play was "The Prince Who Wouldn't Talk", by James Brock. After the performance, a discussion hour took place. One of the first questions came from a youngish, tweedish college professor (or possibly a TA).

"Do you mean to say that 3rd and 4th grade students will really watch this?"

"Oh yes, " I answered, turning on my most professional TV smile. "In fact, just a couple of weeks ago, as the kids were leaving the auditorium, I was directly in front of two boys, ages about 8 and 9. They were discussing the play rather spiritedly, and just before I was out of earshot, I heard the one say, "This sure is cool, to have a TV show right here in school...."

"Curtis", the other boy replied in a withering tone, "that was not a TV show. That was a PLAY, a LIVE PLAY".

"Curtis accepted his correction with grace, I'm happy to say."

The tweedy TA presumed, I suppose, that high

school actors could not hold the interest of sophisticated children who were used to fancy backdrops on TV, synchronized sound, talking animals—that perhaps even the word "Prince" was an anachronism with no meaning for a 20th century child. Ah well...

Both the TA and Myrtle totally missed the point of what was happening in that small stage space: make-believe magic, ideas brought to life by real, alive characters. At least once each season, we would receive fan mail from some of the true believers of make-believe. For example:

Dear Players,

I liked the play. It was Fantastick. What was the formula? I liked Calabad. She was funny. Thank you for the peppermints.
I liked the play. It was funny.
I hope you are doing good. I'm doing good. Thanks for the candy. The play was great.
I liked the play very much It was the best I ever saw so far.
I especially liked the part when they chased each other. That was my favorite part.
Love, Becky

I liked your play. I liked the toy machine the best. I liked the formula H=GBX. I did NOT like the formula H=BBx.

   Your friend Nathan

i LiKED YOUR PLAY.
THE THiNG i DiDN'T LiKE WAS WHEN EVERYONE SCREAMED.
EVERY TiME CALABOD STUCK HER HEAD OUT OF THE DOOR. i STUCK MY TONGUE OUT AT HER.

   CHRiS

Sometimes the mail included thoughts by the principal of the school:

   Thank you very much for bringing the toy factory and a fun-filled play to us. "The Invention" was well presented by the players. We appreciate all your effort.
   I'll pass along the suggestion of many teachers that a little less audience involvement might be considered. While it's fun for them to react, it often becomes a problem to settle them to a level where

everyone can hear, see and enjoy in a
proper manner.

We look forward to having you again
next year.

Ah well, audience participation is not for everyone.
"Puss In Boots" for example won quieter acclaim from its
audiences, and I especially liked this letter from a third
grader:

Dear Actors:

I enjoyed your play Puzz In
Bootz. The princezz waz beautiful and I liked her perzonality
the mozt. I would like to zee
the play again if I could. Thank
you for coming and bezt of all,
for the perfect timing. Right
in the middle of math.

your friend,
Janet M

Now that's a sharp little third-grader.

Sometimes, Bexley Children's Theatre would prepare a seasonal piece, especially for community Christmas events. Before Fort Hunter north of the city became an historic park, complete with Culture Center for special activities, Christmas was celebrated on just one evening of the season, by candlelight, in the parlour of the Museum Mansion.

A German Club from Bexley High School would come to sing carols in German, the language of the frontier in the early 1700's. There would be home baked cakes and cookies and spiced tea. Often there would be a short play, especially for the children present.

On of these December evenings in the early 1970's, the players were late to arrive, The German Carolers sang a few repeat stanzas. Finally, we could hear footsteps on the front porch. The big door swung open, but the players troupe still stood uncertainly just inside the front hallway. I went to meet them.

"Matt", I motioned to their young leader. "Just come inside. There's a place to get ready upstairs."

Still the players remained almost transfixed. I gathered there was a problem. Their director, Matt, a high school senior, had an unusual story to tell. When he had picked up the cast members, he had also picked up some props, and in his haste had included a can of paint by mistake. Cast and crew and props were all packed into the van. The ride might have been uneventful except for the fact that near city line, just five minutes from Fort Hunter, the van bounced over a pothole. The paint can, in turn, had bounced to the floor, its lid springing open. Snowy paint jetted in all directions, particularly onto the gown of the princess.

As this story unfolded, I could already see tracks from a few of the players on the walnut stained hall floor. I could see tiny drips through the yards of pink net of the gown the Princess was carefully holding. Briefly I disappeared to the kitchen for a roll of paper towels. The German Carolers sang some more refrains while I put all the players in a back bedroom of the servants' quarters of the Mansion. Eventually," The Little Toy Soldier" was ready, more or less, to be performed.

At the close of the evening, the Princess revealed to me that the dress had been her Mother's prom gown, but not to worry, her Grandmother would remove the paint. Ah, the optimism of youth. I had visions of a tiny, devoted, white-haired lady bending over the dress, picking paint from the net with a pin, all through the holidays, and perhaps on and on into the New Year.

And now back to the Great Pumpkin and his travels. As I had told you, the pumpkin Walt had found weighed 80 pounds. With the assistance of one other person, Walt could hoist the pumpkin onto the bus and off again. Much of the time, the two persons then rolled–no, SWIVELED–it along.

During the question and answer session with the audience after a performance, it was not Cinderella, nor the Prince, nor the whiney step-sisters who prompted the questions: it was the PUMPKIN. How big is it? Where did you find it? How many pies can you make from a pumpkin that big?

Walt sometimes added a bit of magic to his answers: He had stumbled into the pumpkin one dark night while walking along the uncle's field; the pumpkin was about to be entered into a State Fair, and he pleaded with his uncle to let him have the great pumpkin for the Cinderella Show...

After the fifth presentation of the season, I noticed the one side of the pumpkin was showing signs of wear. There were several bruises, a little curvature where there should not have been. On at least two of the bus trips, the pumpkin had rolled down the bus aisle, knocking into seat supports along the way. And, the weather was turning warmer. Children's Theatre season begins in late March, when often there are still patches of snow along the route to those far distant elementary schools. By late April, days are warmer—the wild dogwood trees and some red buds are in bloom. By early May, the afternoons can be in the 80's, with possibly a thunderstorm threatening as we load and unload the bus.

I was sure the GP was not acclimating well to the warmer times, and I noticed that Walt and his buddy Jeff were finding it more strenuous to hoist and swivel. Clearly, we might have to stretch the properties make-believe, even though the Bexley Arts Festival evening was still up ahead.

"Mrs. J?" I sensed that Walt had come to an important decision. "I think we will have to discard the Great Pumpkin. There's an odd feel about it now, and sort of an odd odor, too."

"It's OK, Walt. I'll ask the custodian to pick it up for disposal after school tomorrow."

I filed my request with the Chief Custodian.

Tessa, an assistant custodian who always swept out my room at the end of the day, vacuuming the carpet on the speaker's platform and setting the window blinds at regulation length (as decreed by the Principal), talked with me the next day about the Great Pumpkin.

"I think, Mrs. J, we'll need a dolly and a number of green plastic bags", Tessa said.

She went in search of the dolly and came back with a fresh box of 30 gallon green plastic bags. No student from the audiences had ever asked, how many bags would it take to carry a cut-up 80-pound pumpkin? Tessa did not have a large knife; I secured one from the depths of my utility cupboard. I kept a large, not very sharp knife for cutting sheet cakes when the Drama Club had a holiday party. I started cutting up the Pumpkin. About forty minutes later I was still cutting and chopping.

Tessa said, "Now just take your time, Mrs. J., I'll go sweep the two rooms next door." I had already filled three bags and secured them with knotted ties. Two room sweepings later, I finished off the fifth 30-gallon bags. The pumpkin was very smelly, its insides a fantasy collection of molds. The shell, unbelievably, was still somewhat firm, otherwise my dull knife would not have succeeded with the execution. The dolly was large enough for the five filled plastic bags. Tessa called on the intercom for a male custodian to come down to Room 17 to push.

Near 5 pm on a late May afternoon, I watched the last of what had been the Great Pumpkin, as he was pushed from my room and down the dim hallway to the trash holding bin–the last length of his travels.

"The world of reality has
its limits, the world of imagination
is boundless."

                    -Jean-Jacques Rousseau

The Widest River in the World

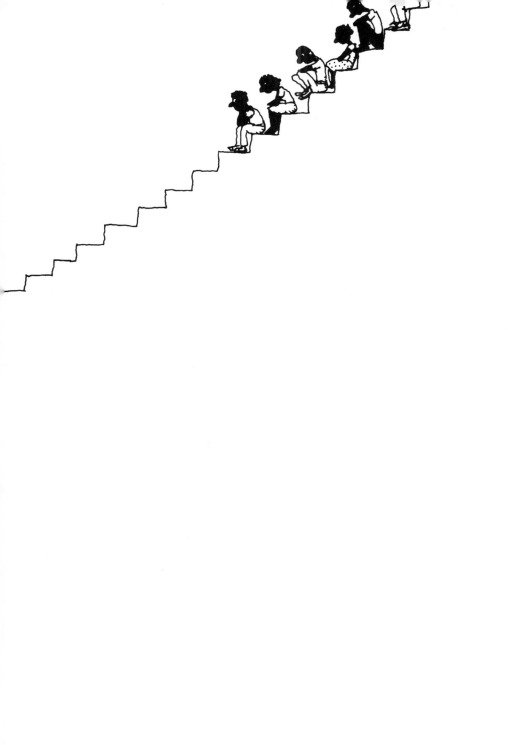

In the latter part of the 70's our city became a disembarkation center for Vietnamese immigrants. Bexley Hills High School was to have about 20 families enrolling students from grades 10 to 12. Eventually, some Laotian boat people arrived as well as Cambodians and a number of South Korean families.

Earlier on, in the 60's, as more and more engineers from India were hired by state government, South Shore District would usually have about 30 Indian students enrolled at various grade levels. By the late 80's a number of Hispanic Americans, especially newcomers from Puerto Rico, were enrolled at Bexley.

So who was missing? Black students. Once in awhile I would see black students at elementary schools where we presented Children's Theatre plays, but in high school, where there were almost 1800 students when I arrived, we had one black student—a boy who regarded himself as a black activist. Then for a time, we had two girls, whose political points of view were never revealed. By the time I retired. In 1993, there were five black students—one was a ballerina and musician, one was an activist headed for the ministry, one was inclined to doze off in Speech Class, one was often in speech contests, and one was president of the Freshman Class.

In the greater city area there was a 12 to 15% Afro-American population. So where were the Afro-American children in school? They were mostly across the wide, wide river, enrolled in district schools on the NORTH shore. I had Bexley students tell me they never went into the city; they didn't shop downtown, nor use the State Library. They had been to the Capital building once, on a school field trip. They had never been to the Memorial Day Arts Festival, held at River Front Park, nor to the fireworks display and Boat Parade at the River Front on Labor Day, (they could, of course, see the fireworks from the South Shore side of the river...)

My second contest season at Bexley I had the broadcasting students prepare a documentary entitled, "Open Housing on the South Shore", to explore the reasons who so few black persons bought or rented homes in the area. The leader of the group preparing the tape interviewed several realtors, the one black Bexley student, and the President of the local NAACP for the greater city area, Michael Boyer. The tape won the runner-up award at the State Speech Tournament. A few weeks later, I happened to be at a State Museum gathering where I saw the NAACP president. For a few minutes I chatted with him, then said, "Mr. Boyer, I'm not sure if you received the word or not, but our broadcasting tape, "Open Housing on the South Shore", won the second top award at the contest. We thank you for the interview time."

Mr. Boyer gave me a very direct look, and after a moment or so said, "I did this for the children. Yes, I did this for the children."

Doubtless, what he didn't add was, I could care less about the award, even less about the realtors' remarks, and no thanks for your thank-you.

I understood that probably my remarks had sounded

patronizing, or at least I should not have mentioned the award.

It was soon after, April 4, 1968, that Martin Luther King, Jr. was assassinated. As was the custom at Bexley, when a national figure died, there was a brief memorial service held in the auditorium. On the afternoon of the service for Dr. King, the Principal, Mr. Anderson, before introducing my Choral Readers who would present several poems, leaned heavily on the lectern, was silent for a few moments, and then said, "In recent months you probably have seen the Protests on television. Among the leaders, the man who was probably one of the better persons of this group is the person whose memory we recall today." I could not believe what I was hearing.

Mr. Anderson continued. "Whatever you think about all of this, we expect you to be courteous at this time, to listen to the Choral Readers and to the music by the orchestra ensemble."

The twenty-minute program continued and after its completion, the students went to their respective classes.

Two days later, at the hairdressers, one of the operators, a Bexley graduate, brought up the subject of the assassination, and said rather loudly to be sure that all the customers heard.

"You know, at Bexley High there was a memorial service for King, and there were teachers at the back of the auditorium, holding the doors shut so that no one could leave." I made no comment. She was not talking to me nor had she ever worked on my hair. Many times over since then, I've thought how wrong it was that I did not comment. It was quite true that teachers, especially male gym teachers, always stood at the back of the auditorium for an assembly program. They had no home rooms, no normal size classes—they were anxious to get away to a practice session of coaching as soon as possible. No student tried to leave during that memorial program.

In class news discussions no student had ever commented that we should not have had a memorial program. No student commented either about the Principal's poor introduction of the program. Perhaps many of the students, like the Principal and the beautician, did not understand at all that they were living in one of the most significant times of their country's history. Perhaps what happened three years later at Bexley in September, 1971, came as a real shock to students, alumni and Mr. Anderson. I felt no surprise.

On a mild mid-September evening in 1971, my husband Bob and daughter Vicki, walked over to Bexley to see the football game—Bexley was playing the favored visiting team, a mostly black team from across the river. The teams were not playing for a championship, nor even a playoff berth. There were about 13,000 fans in attendance; in those days, parents and friends would reserve the same seats, season after season. The stadium would be filled to capacity, and on the visitors side, a game with an archrival in the Central League would fill every seat.

Perhaps it was the hazy mildness of the weather, more likely the booze that came in surreptitiously with a number of the fans. When Bob and Vicki arrived home (about 20 minutes walking distance from the school), they commented on the size of the crowd, the half-time show, and then Bob said,

"We left a few minutes early to avoid the mob. Bexley had a 17-14 lead with just 25 seconds remaining..."

Now Bob had played football all through his high school days in a New Jersey school; he had even played some football in college; he was a faithful watcher of football on TV. By leaving the South Shore field two minutes early, it's true he had avoided a mob, but he and Vicki had also missed the mêlée or call it a race riot if you wish, that was to have ramifications for the school and all of the teams in the Central League for the next quarter of a century.

What had happened—on the final two plays of the game, with Bexley at a 17-14 lead, with just 25 seconds remaining, the opposing team had one last chance: Capitol City's Frank Martin took a pass from Duke Huston 50 yards to the Bexley 26 as time expired. On the final two plays of the game, players pushed and shoved one another after the whistle had blown the play dead. When time expired, spectators from both schools poured onto the field. The fracas involved about 300 people, fighting lasted about 40 minutes. Six people, including a county sheriff, were sent to the hospital; many others suffered minor injuries. Police from five South Shore communities, plus 15 state troopers, were called in to restore order.

Three days later a neighboring regional school withdrew from the Central League, "due to the reason of public safety of the children"; the next day, schools announced the banning of night games. Bexley was soon to drop out of the Central League, both football and basketball. Bexley moved to the South-Central League, where no school was regarded as much "opposition".

Within five years there was no longer a Central League—the team from Capitol City that had had so many fine players had no league at all until into the 80's. And as late as 1992, just before the year I retired, I was having coffee with an old broadcasting friend. "And where did you say you are still teaching?" she asked.

"At Bexley Hills High School, the South Shore District."

"Oh..." was Dorothy's only comment.

Suppose the scene had played out otherwise: the Central League members had held together. Suppose they had backed the Capitol City School Board President, who blamed trouble-makers and drop-outs for the violence and warned, "All persons bent on trouble, even those criminal elements who caused our recent problems, STAY AWAY FROM OUR FOOTBALL GAMES!"

Suppose there had been public apologies from both teams! A series of open meetings at both schools.

One effort at least on the part of student government from Capitol City was made—a group of their students presented an assembly program at Bexley, with music and dancing and narrative to help us come to better understanding of the two races—to make the river seem a little less wide.

No program prepared at Bexley was sent to Capitol City. And although through theater and contest work I was able to have small numbers of students visit schools in the region, as well as the state university where our annual tournament was held and Bexley students could see the performances of black students while black students could debate and perform for white students—this was not nearly enough experience, and it surely had far smaller numbers than sports events.

At this point in time, one of my finest contest participants was also an excellent actress, Children's Theatre director and straight "A" student—Emily Austin. A Senior, she was going to receive the Speech Department award for excellence at Commencement. It was my policy, if a student were to be receiving such an award, he or she would also be one of the two students chosen as commencement speakers to represent the department. You will recall that the other two students were the FACULTY chosen speaker and the STUDENT chosen speaker.

When I submitted my list to Mr. Anderson in late April, he looked at it for at least a full minute. Then he leaned back in his desk chair, removed his glasses, polished his glasses, then pushed back his chair, got up, walked over to his office door and closed it. I was still standing in front of his desk.

"Sit down please, Lillian". I would have been a lot less uneasy if he had called me "Mrs. Juditz". There was some kind of trouble here, but I was really not prepared for what he said next. I sat down.

"Emily Austin will not be a commencement speaker."

"Oh, for what reason?"

"I'm sure you're aware her boyfriend is colored."

"I am aware she dates a black student. I've met him and talked with him several times, when he came to play rehearsals. Matt is enrolled at Bishop Newman...he's a Senior headed for college.

Mr. Anderson sucked on his glasses frame. "That's beside the point. It's not debatable."

I waited a few seconds. "Are you also going to prevent Emily from receiving the Speech Award?"
"I'm not in a position to do that."

I noticed Mr. Anderson was now twirling a pen, he did not look at me.

"Mr. Anderson, I am very sorry about all this, both sorry and puzzled. I will find a speaker replacement for Emily, and I will give you the name very soon. I left his office and did not bother to close the door.

I was so angry at this offensive chunk of humanity. And totally infuriated with myself!!!! Why couldn't I do something??? Maybe if I had gone first to the commencement speaker coach, maybe he could have brought pressure to Anderson? I doubted that—Louis Sutton talked a good fight—I'd never known him to be in a good fight.

The Superintendent? Remember, a few years down the track he turned out to be the anti-Semitic one; maybe instinctively I knew there was little hope with him. The Union? Ten years later the Union would have plenty of strength; it was still low profile, and still could be joined for

$20, (up from the original $15.00). I had to admit I never made waves. I was never transferred. I was never a threat.

Later that day, I finally reasoned: Anderson would be Anderson the rest of his life. He had come from the coal regions, (unkindly behind his back, people would call him a "coal cracker"). He would have been opposed to Irish, Croatians, Serbians, Hungarians. BUT he would never have dared oppose a "boyfriend" from any of these groups: black was obvious. He held "black" responsible for changing his beloved sports league—that was perhaps the strongest reason for his rejection of Emily. I also found myself thinking: none of us at Bexley is free from the Anderson taint. I've lived in this community since 1960—only twice has a black person been in my home; only once have I been in a black person's home, and that was the North Shore home of our choreographer, Norman Hoff. Musical after musical Norman served as our dance director, our choreo-grapher for the large group scenes with split-second timing and he polished off our production numbers. Serving under four different musical directors, Norman Hoff brought the magic to our musicals.

On one occasion, when we were working on a very difficult jazz interpretation, Norman invited all the show directors (I was involved in script study and costumes), to his home for discussion, refreshments—and to assure continuing good will, I suspect.

I was also thinking—with just a little more effort and imagination, I could have invited guest black actors from other schools to appear in our main stage plays. I was so careful to be "politically correct" and not turn white-face into black-face—I should have used that energy to make a few phone calls to other coaches to find some black students who would agree to be guest actors. As some black students used to say on contest days at Bexley, "We always lock our car doors when we come into your area, but we are always glad to come!"

To this day in the South Shore District, with its 80 million dollar budget, its two crown jewel high schools, its four handsome middle schools, its twelve far-flung elementary schools, its five thousand students, its 650 teachers and multiple admin staff members, there are still no black teachers, no black coaches. It may well be the problem of Open Housing is no closer to being solved now than it was forty years ago, but teachers and coaches and administrative personnel can be sought out and hired and encouraged to help diversity unite us rather than divide us.

In the Spring of 1993 I finally had one last chance: a local church just down the street from my home wanted to have a one-act play as part of their annual Spring Fling evening. The theme for the group's study that year had been diversity—would I be able to help them?

Immediately, I knew which play and which actors. "Open Admission" by Shirley Lauro, "Open Admission," the one-act version "centers, on the explosive relationship between a Black college student, Calvin, and his White instructor, Dr. Alice Stockwell. Calvin, studying at City College of New York under the 'Open Admissions Plan' for minorities, believes he's being betrayed by his teacher who has operated on a double standard, shuffling him through "B's" irrespective of the quality of his work, while concentrating all real efforts on White students.

I would ask the president of the Freshmen Class, Carl James to play Calvin, and from my Senior actresses, I would ask Nancy Soder, who had played Miss Sullivan in "The Miracle Worker, to take the role of Dr. Stockwell- Both agreed even though the event did not take place until mid-May, when Final Exams were coming up and the "final events" of all kinds of school groups were taking place. James and Nancy were both Honor students, and both were A+ in reliability—no late starts at rehearsal, no skipping rehearsals.

The evening of May 16th was clear and cool (always a plus for a church play, where stages are rarely air-conditioned and the lighting panel is in a snug little space with not much breathing room). Those of us involved with the play had agreed to forgo dinner, to allow plenty of time for make-up and stage setting. We knew the audience would be at least a hundred persons; hearing their chatter from the other side of the velvet curtains, they seemed to be in a fine Spring Fling mood and they were a really great audience, their applause very generous. I had been asked to present, at the close of the play, 30 minutes of comment for video-taping, regarding the playwright's intent and my feelings about the message of the play. I was not at all sure how much more "message" this fine audience would be prepared to take. Nancy and James were invited to have dessert at one of the side tables, and they stayed on to listen to my comments. All of the audience stayed on—it was amazing. Surely this group's study of diversity had made impact.

Since that May evening almost ten years ago, I have collected a file of articles on how kids can learn about diversity, tolerance, fighting bigotry. Dr. Debra Van Ausdale, coauthor of "The First R: How Children Learn Race and Racism" insists parents need to teach acceptance and tolerance early. Age three is not too young to introduce basic facts such as skin color, eye shape and hair texture—things children visualize and can touch. Some of the steps Dr. Van Ausdale recommends to parents include:

```
Actively form friendships with adults
who belong to other ethnic and racial
groups.

Recognize your child's curiosities and
abilities to explore the world with a
sense of fairness.

Point out instances of everyday racism
and discuss them, even with a very
young child.

Take your child to multiracial events
and multicultural activities in your
community.
```

Encourage your child to make friends
with children of many racial and ethnic
groups, and then incorporate these
friends and their families into your
family's activities.

Encourage children to read books that
offer stories they can identify with
and that actively promote greater
understanding of all people.

"If you don't like the way the
world is, you change it. You just
do it one step at a time."

Marian Wright Edelman
Founder and president,
Children's Defense Fund

First Things First: VALUES

During my third year at Bexley–the end of the 60's when the enrollment was holding at about 1800 students–there were temporary classrooms in the lobbies, and one day I found myself monitoring a study hall, directly opposite the courtyard.

In the center of the courtyard, on a plot of grass raised about five feet from the ground level concrete of the yard, there was a very handsome blue spruce tree, perhaps twenty feet tall, elegant in its perfection. I stared at the blue spruce for twenty minutes or so. Then suddenly, I realized it had a problem: near the trunk, in the very center of the stately tree, a vine was growing. A noxious weed? An even more noxious poison ivy? A parasitic weed tree?–as one tree consultant termed our neighbor's "plantings".

I thought to myself, I must alert the chief custodian, the person who hires the lawn crew. I left a note that day in the chief custodian's mailbox, and a copy in the assistant principal's mailbox.

November 14

I noticed today (while I was monitoring a study hall in Room T-4) that a substantial vine is growing in the blue spruce tree in the center of the courtyard. This will do some real harm to the tree and should be removed before winter sets in (early December).

Thanks for your attention,

Lillian M. Judity

I checked and watched and waited. I watched and waited for two weeks or so–the vine was still there. I wondered to whom I now ought to send a note.

The first substantial snow fell early that year, December 10th; the courtyard was swiftly drifted over. The snow hid the weed, the handsome blue spruce stood tall and lovely–some birds flittered in and out its branches when sunshine returned. I thought, come Spring I'll find the right person to talk to.

Come Spring, the noxious weed thing was still there, a little larger than before. No one had ever acknowledged my note. There really is, I think, an analogy here about the values of Bexley and the South Shore community: if something beautiful is often ignored, especially when it's in need of some help, then it follows that other problems of the school will have the same fate.

It was Popovi Da, a member of the San Ildefonso Indian tribe of New Mexico, an eminent ceramist who said in a talk for the School of American Research:

"Our (Native American) values are indwelling and dependent on time and space unmeasured. This in itself is beauty. Our first great value is our trusteeship of nature, and this is beauty also. Then there is an order and direction of our lives, a unity, the ability to share the joy of sharing, creativeness and minimum competition. This too is beauty".

Earlier this year, I was re-reading a number of letters I had sent to my daughter Vicki when she was first away at college—she had saved these and returned them to me just before her graduation near the end of the 70's.

I re-learned some interesting news items from that Bexley era: a Homecoming Queen had stuffed the ballot box to win her honors; a transfer student had thrown a cherry bomb into my room to avoid taking a test; in a third instance, I had had to pass instead of fail a girl at the request of both her counselor and psychiatrist—the student had failed the course on purpose because she wanted to go back to her other female speech teacher with whom she was infatuated.

I began thinking of these instances as evidence of confused values. But on the other hand I remembered also that at the end of the 80's when my husband Bob had died during Christmas vacation, and I returned to classes on January 4th, the assistant principal immediately warned me, "You might find some students very unfeeling, they might make some very inappropriate remarks." The first two students I met that day, as I was removing wraps from the windowsill plants and adding fresh water–Alex Beck and Jerome Fenton both came into the room a little early–Alex came right over to the window.

"Mrs. J.–are you alright?"

"I'm doing well, Alex, and it's good of you to ask."

A little later, into the class time, I took a few minutes to mention that–my husband had been an officer in the Regional Toastmasters Club, that he had always felt public speaking was one of the best things that had ever happened to him, and further, that training about making speeches had really earned for him his position as an official with the State Department of Transportation.

None of the 170 students I met that week had anything inappropriate or unkind to say. One 14-year-old boy did ask my age, (he was looking for a step-mother I learned), and when I told him my age–58–he commented. "Oh really. No, I guess not. My Dad is 41."

I understood. I was not quite as prepared for the chemistry teacher's conversation. This teacher had been known as the "bachelor chem teacher" for some time. Somehow the subject of age was brought up; among several of us at lunch, and Mr. Bachelor said (when learning that I was 58), "Why you're old enough to be my mother!"

While we're still here on this risky topic of age, I really believe that a major part of the problem in the search for values is the "divorce" between the ages. The young, the old, the various degrees of time between the two are carefully separated–learning, working, socializing. Age divides us like concrete. And because this is our condition, it becomes very difficult to pass on our values.

And our culture. The lack of communication between the ages tends to make us substitute work for cultural activity within the family. To use the term loosely, "Cultural activity" would be the Little League Game after school, and parents do get to these events. But it's problematical what values are being passed along when Mom and Dad are yelling for a home run and will obviously be going back to their car with their noses out of joint because they couldn't handle the competition.

At the annual holiday concert, a substantial number of parents will arrive late, but in time for the numbers their sons and daughters will sing; others will leave early (noisily) after a certain segment of the concert is over. It could be argued the busy parents did show up; showing up is not the same as respectfully listening to a program from start to finish, sharing the beauty of an event with other parents and students.

It has more or less the value flavor of our Chairman-of-the-English-Department, who always headed for the shore at 12:01 on the final day of the school year. Which meant that he wouldn't attend the small luncheon that had been set up to honor the department's retiring teachers. I often speculated: did he have to leave at that time to avoid late afternoon shore traffic? Did he have to leave at that time because he preferred to eat lunch at the fast food places on the Turnpike? Did he have to leave at that time to meet the deadline for registration wherever he was staying at the shore?...or was he thinking, who in his right mind wants to go to anybody's retirement luncheon?...WHO THE HELL CARES????

There were other skewed values examples: to relate a few—a guidance counselor always discouraged students from applying to an ivy-league school, because he thought ivy-league schools were snotty. The son of the assistant principal happened to be dating one of my speech students. She and some other friends were chatting with me one day near the end of class time; somehow we got on the subject of Italy. I mentioned that I had been there some years ago, had enjoyed the trip so much. And she asked me, "Why would you want to go to Italy?" While you ponder over that question, be generous enough to allow for the fact that the girl was about sixteen, probably thought of vacation time as "down the shore"—like the English Chairman.

Now consider this situation: During the year that was to be my last at Bexley, I promoted and helped organize OPERA OUTREACH. This was a ten-day special mini course for both our high schools at South Shore. It was founded by a former opera singer of our area. The guest lecturers were well- trained in their fields: music literature, architecture, set design, costume research. The whole idea was to encourage the student (attending voluntarily) to understand the career opportunities in the world of opera-professionally (as at the Met) or locally, as with our non-professional state companies.

I had obtained permission from the District Office to run this mini-course. There was no charge to the school district a number of local businesses were picking up the tab, which was a very nominal fee. The program proceeded as planned, the students were responsive, even the bussing of the group of students from the sister high school came off on schedule.

At the culmination of the course, there was an hour-long program of operatic selections; three of the performers were Bexley grads. Just one thing was missing: the Principal of Bexley (the blackmailing one) chose not to be present. His introductory remarks for the program were performed by his second assistant. I checked. The Principal was not ill that day; he was not scheduled to appear in court; he was not meeting with the contractors who were going to lay the Astroturf in the stadium–(his first assistant was doing that).

To this day I don't know where Mr. Harvey was holed up, but I readily understood where his values were (not) coming from.

In an earlier chapter of this book, "Those Who Fear Books", I had mentioned the efforts of the Christian fundamentalists to defeat the proposed plan for OBE–Outcome Based Education. What is outcome-based education? OBE is an approach to education which is based on three beliefs: All children can learn and succeed. Success breeds success. Schools determine the conditions of success. The curriculum in an OBE system emphasizes roles such as citizen, family member, worker and lifelong learner.

At that point, the Christian fundamentalists began to prepare their attack: their justification for this action was–the school is attempting to take over the role of the parents. Of course the irony of the issue–OBE comes out of a behavioral science tradition half a century old: state what you want students to be able to do in measurable terms, then design curriculum that lets them learn how to do it.

One example of how the OBE firestorm derailed a section of curriculum that had the title under citizenship, "Appreciating and Understanding Others". All students demonstrate the ability to interact with others on the basis of their individual merits and, without discrimination because of their race, religion, ethnicity, gender disability, lifestyle or socioeconomic status. This outcome was reworked to read and be approved by the state legislature, "Appreciating and understanding others section deleted from final regulation."

Alden J. Moe, as dean of the College of Education at Lehigh University wrote:" We must share our values about respect, honesty, democracy, tolerance, acceptance, morality and our obligation to care for others. In an article first written for the Allentown Morning Call, he said, "It has been argued that for the last 30 years the role of character education and the teaching of values has been diminishing or even has disappeared in our nation's schools...From Bosnia-Herzegovina to Somalia to the streets of America's cities and suburbs, we see violent evidence of our value distorted world. And while education cannot offer all the answers, public and private schools are critical to under-standing, moderating and re-directing hostile human capa-bilities." Dean Moe was writing this in June 1994. In the years since then there have been numerous writers decry-ing the current state of culture and politics in America.

There are three books I suggest you read and rec-ommend to your friends and neighbors. The first one is by Sara Lawrence-Lightfoot, professor of education at Harvard University. In her new book, "Respect" (Perseus Books), she answers the question, " What can schools do to create a climate of respect?" She writes, we need to have smaller schools and smaller class sizes." She's right in the camp with my student Martin Blair who was "shot down" by our school board for suggesting the same thing. And Professor Lawrence Lightfoot went on to say, "We also need to make schools like the old neighborhood, where all adults felt they could punish or reward all the kids."

Answering a second important question, How can educators create classrooms that are places where respect grows? First, get to know the students through their work; do a lot of writing. Classrooms need to be safe environ-ments where kids can say what they're feeling and thinking. It's wrong for a teacher's value system to dominate. A good-teacher will open up the discussion. It's all about dialogue, testing our ideas, learning to ask good questions.

The second book is by the author and Yale Law pro-fessor, Stephen Carter, "Civility Manners, Morals and the Etiquette of Democracy. He writes: Civility is not simply a useful politeness; it's a moral issue that deals with how we view and relate to each other and will determine the future of our democratic society. It often requires us to put aside our own interests and desires for the benefit of others, which is what civilization is all about. What we need is a society that recognizes we have shared obligations to young people for a morally coherent world, a world in which they don't get mixed messages, in which there are some aspects of morality that adults all share and model in their lives.

Probably his most dramatic example for a teacher of communication is: "eighty-nine percent of public school teachers say they regularly face abusive language from students. Language has power Carter explores in his book the power of words both to heal and to hurt. "Words can wound...the way we use words matters. There is the way fighting words pervade our language, the way we tend to demonize political opponents, the language we use to cut off discussion altogether. And then there is the language of the marketplace that encourages us to get what we want and do whatever we want."

For your third book, I hope you will read "For Common Things: Irony, Trust and Commitment in America Today", written by Jedediah Purdy. Purdy was home schooled on a hillside farm in West Virginia before he attended Harvard. Merle Rubin, who reviewed his book for the Christian Science Monitor wrote, "He shows a sophisticated understanding of the various factors that have led many Americans to feel that politics is a dirty word. Purdy perceives a widespread attitude of ironic indifference, as citizens retreat, not only from taking an active part in politics but even from talking and thinking about public issues.

"Not only in America" Purdy writes, "but throughout the world, there is a dangerous and utterly erroneous belief that politics should stand back and let economics do its work, But the proliferation of MacDonald's fast food joints is no guarantee of human rights", Allowing the marketplace to do its work in Purdy's home state has resulted in the coal industry's removal of mountaintops and despoliation of the environment.

When I send along this chapter for my daughter to read, I know exactly what she's going to say: "Mom, it's really useless to tell a reader what else to read—readers are already snowed under. You'll be lucky if many readers get this far back in your book. Wrap up this chapter with one last good example that YOU know about...

I thought for a few moments." Vicki do you remember Carolyn Emory?"

"Colonel Emory's daughter? The little Eurasian girl who was nominated to be a Beauty Queen? I thought you said you never knew the whole story..."

"I didn't, until about four weeks ago. I learned quite by accident how the whole event came about—who was responsible."

I'm sorry to say it's a Bexley "values story", the saddest of its kind, and the same kind of thing has probably happened in hundreds of high schools across the country.

That autumn of 1974, Carolyn was beginning her Senior year at Bexley. Her Dad had been transferred from a base in Texas. There was no mother. Carolyn was in an Honors Class. She was short; her skinny hair was dark, skin olive. I don't know if everybody knew she was Eurasian as soon as they met, but she did look somewhat different. It so happened there was a macho football player, a vice-president of the Senior class who thought it would be a good joke to nominate Carolyn as one of the eight homecoming Beauty Queens. And that's exactly what he did. And although the football clown might not have been aware of the fact, when the list of nominees went down to the desk of the Class Dean's secretary, the jaw of that lady dropped a couple of inches. She went immediately to the desk of the Assistant Principal: a number of topics were quickly covered—she's going to need an appropriate gown, and a hair appointment, and make-up instruction. She's going to need an ESCORT!

"Oh", said the Assistant Principal. "Well, we don't have much time—Homecoming is two weeks away. Who did the nomination?

The secretary to the Class Dean lowered her voice, and for twenty-seven years thereafter that name was probably the very best kept secret at Bexley.

"You said he was a macho football player," prompted Vicki. "Yes, and in time he was in real estate locally, and in some more years he became the Justice of the Peace, and when he had a much better office down the street from the school, he was elected to the School Board. When he was a Board Director he often did not show up at meetings. He was Director at the time of our strike in '88.

I paused a moment. "I'm afraid, Vicki, we didn't know enough about teaching values.

"Teaching about values means opening the minds of young people to the alternative value systems of differing thinkers. Ex'posing them to the fresh winds of doctrine...

-Sydney Harris

The Winds of Change

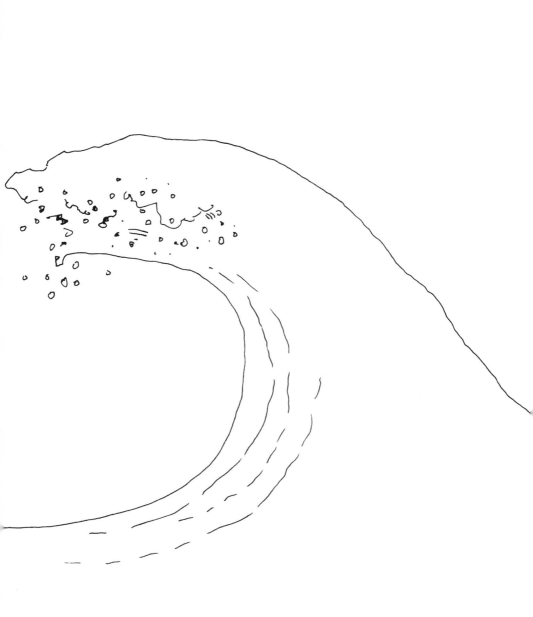

Well, here it is. Chapter Twenty, the last chapter of the book. Will you read it? I don't recall which famous author it was, but he said he had almost NEVER read the last chapter of any book...(and he did not reveal his reason).

From 1966 to 1993, the years I was teaching, REFORM in education was often the topic of focus. In my family of career teachers I don't recall this kind of focus throughout the 40's to early 60's, but then the War had put hold-on many parts of life: in 1942, for example our biggest concern was bomb drills. We were taught how to squiggle under our desks. We had a suitcase filled with toys and games, which we were taught to move rapidly down the hallway to a safer sturdier area of the sixty-year old building.

In the years I was learning, from 1935 to 1950, I count five teachers as memorable and absolutely essential to my education. The first was Miss Noble, (her real name), my 4th grade teacher who had bookcases all around her room (there was elementary, even in a well-to-do district in a medium size Eastern city).

Miss Noble invited me to read all of her books, on class time, at my own speed. When I came to the last book-on the-last shelf, she invited me to start over. Miss Noble taught me the love of reading.

My 8th grade civics teacher taught me how to put together a newspaper celebrating the history of the city. He taught me how to write, how to choose words, how to describe places and people.

In High School, my biology teacher introduced me to a special world of nature. I had lived always in the country, on a farm, but wild nature was passing me by—my biology teacher taught me ecology, conservation, the significance of the food chain before any of these terms were household words. And she taught me how to illustrate my poems and stories of wild things.

In college, it was both my drama coach and my speech coach who gave me the insight to explore the history of theatre, the freedom to create Clytemnestra as well as First Lady from my own understanding, and finally to choose broadcasting as my first career.

You will understand that all of this had nothing to do with OBE, VOUCHERS, CHARTER SCHOOLS (although state law did allow me to pay tuition and go to the city school instead of a rural school). Testing? No, this was all before SAT'S and the national testing in grades 4-8-11. The high school was much too large for today's recommendation—2700 students, classes of 32 to 40. But there was also an 8-page large size newspaper published every week, a choir, a band, a one hundred piece orchestra, main stage plays and musicals and sports.

As I was leaving the teaching profession in the early 90's the biggest topic of reform was OBE (outcome based education, which I told you more about than you cared to know in earlier chapters), Let me tell you now my favorite OBE STORY.

We were all gathered together one early Spring day in the Bexley Library. Staff and three admin members and the chairmen of the various departments. Mr. Harvey, the Principal, was prepared to conduct the meeting. Emory

Lillian Juditz

Dodson, Chairman of Social Studies, meaning American History (Civil War), current events and a smattering of World Cultures, was sitting near the back of the assembled groups. Mr. Harvey called the meeting to order, and as he did so, Emory strode to the speaker's table, superbly upstaging Mr. Harvey (remember he's the blackmailing principal). Emory, facing all of us, is saying, "I want you all to know that in our department at least the one teaching tool we really need is a set of new maps. There's an extra cost involved here (and now the room is totally quiet) but surely this is our greatest need. And I personally think each of us in charge of departments should be able to recognize what is our-greatest need.

In the next six seconds, Mr. Harvey must have experienced something like a lifetime flashing before his eyes—the thousands of dollars and man-hours spent on sending the OBE FACT FINDING COMMITTEE to four different states. He then cleared his throat, rose and thanked Mr. Dodson for his comments and launched into his talk, "The New Paradigm That is OBE."

A few months later, the cover story of Parade Magazine was "Let's ask the students what the schools need". The 16-year-old boy, Pete Henyan, in the center of the cover was quoted, "What we need at our school is MAPS. Up-to-date easy-to-read maps." Bexley's Emory Dodson was indeed vindicated. And he was still far enough away from retirement that he probably did get to use his new set of maps.

Other "reforms" at Bexley recently I discovered that one of the District's finest English teachers was now employed wholly as a Teacher of the Taking of Tests–the SAT's, the standardized tests for the college bound. A teacher of English Literature, a teacher who has the skill to interpret the writings of fine authors to students who will benefit for a lifetime, who will never be bored, lonely, dull–simply because they love to read. A woman similar to Miss Noble, the teacher I was describing at the beginning of this chapter.

Teach for a test? Add more tests? To what purpose? And saddest of all to think about: closing out a fine teaching career by teaching someone how to take a test? This is as wrong as the maneuvers of the blackmailing principal.

By now I'm sure you realize that I do not think REFORM is to be found in a plan with a new label, nor in a certain size building of state-of-the-art design, nor in standardization of texts and testing. The famous private or schools of the Bruderhof Communities in the U.S. and England have got rid of all their computers and TV's. Looking at the results after three years (1999 to 2002) they report the following: the children have thrown off their passivity and have become more creative; class projects involved whole classes and their teachers; in place of surfing the net for facts and figures on the Hudson River, the third and fourth graders researched together in books, made a field trip to the river and saw the rapids that blocked Henry Hudson's route north; crafts have resurged–pottery, painting, metal work at the forge; music and singing have acquired new vigor; and the children are plain happier.

You will argue, of course, that children need to learn computer skills for today's world. True. And at the Bruderhof

Schools 9th graders undergo an intensive keyboarding course. With this behind them, they will rapidly pick up computer commands and operations, IF THEY HAVE BEEN ALLOWED TO DEVELOP ALL THEIR FACULTIES AT THEIR OWN SPEED THROUGH THEIR GRADE SCHOOL YEARS. (In this last sentence, capitalized, lies the reason why the computers and TV's were abandoned: children need their childhood to unfold into the persons they are meant to be).

What else for "reform"? I think each teacher should really love the subject at whatever level it is to be taught. The teacher may love the children, too, but I prefer the word "Respect". Respect the children and their ideas and their performance. Once, early on in my time of teaching I had a student who had a learning difficulty. She introduced me to John Updike's poem, "A Scarf of Birds" She had met John Updike in a bookstore where the author was autographing copies of this poem.

I have had students of every degree of intellect and ability. Before I was a teacher I would have scoffed at the idea an LD student could introduce me to something I would remember a lifetime. Today, I never see a flock of birds... I see a SCARF of birds, sometimes even a SHAWL.

The final time I was evaluated in my teaching career, it was again by Mr. Harvey (lucky me!) one of the student speakers in class that day was not an LD student, but he had a handicap. In his head was a silver plate–the surgery allowed him to recover from a very serious head injury. His speech was not impaired but he had trouble with fluency. He used his note cards frequently; sometimes he had to pause a little longer to collect his thoughts. But he did communicate his ideas to the audience, and the audience appreciated his ideas.

Well, not all of his audience. Mr. Harvey confided to me that the boy was not very well -prepared; he needed more practice.

"Do you know?" I questioned Mr. Harvey; "He has a silver plate in his head? He is, to a degree, handicapped."

Mr. Harvey pursed his lips and said, "Oh".

Yes, in considering school reforms, I would be very cautious about the selection of middle managers, and surely, if there were 112 candidates for a top level manager, like Superintendent, I would urge the Board to do some research on the backgrounds of these persons.

Before you decide that this chapter could get very stormy with the gusty winds of educational reform, from the hundreds of articles, books, lectures, interviews there are several I've chosen to stir your curiosity to lead you into some interesting conversations with relatives and neighbors.

First, there is the CIRCLE School, a capital city area private school whose core values are equality and self-direction. There are no teachers, no grades, no classes. The school is operated by a system of democratic self-governance. "We create an environment that is rich and safe, within constraints that allows the children to choose the things they will spend their time on", explained staff member Jim Rietmulder. "Kids know what they want and need to learn." Staff members and students are part of the governmental organization called their School Meeting. Each member has one vote and the majority rules. A chairperson is responsible for the weekly meetings which are run according to "Robert's Rules of Order."

Among educators-for-reform there is John Taylor Gatto, who published his first book "Dumbing Us Down" back in 1991 and since then has traveled 1.4 million miles in America and seven foreign countries to observe home schooling. About 2 million people have in effect set up private labs in education. John Gatto asks, what makes a good school? That the school part is de-emphasized. You have to believe that everybody wants the best, wants to learn, to have meaningful work to do.

I was impressed to learn from him that he taught 13 year olds from inner city using the same text and method he used at Columbia and Cornell. He never accepted second-rate work without showing a kid why it was second rate. When I taught Julius Caesar to 14-year-old Track Three students, (a group of nine that included seven girls, one boy from the Laotian Boat People and one male parolee "who lived around",) I was so pleased to discover their interest, partly because there were Bexley teachers of senior honor students who said," I wouldn't dream of trying to teach Shakespeare to kids like that. They just butcher the language. I can't take it." Oh well…

Currently the educator you will be hearing about most is Leon Botstein, President of Bard College. Bard College and New York's Board of Education have paired up to open a high school where college replaces the boredom of the ordinary public high school senior year. In other words this experiment allows students to compress four years of high school into two and them complete two years of college by the age of 18. The students involved in this experiment are all volunteers. We await the findings.

What can you discuss about reform in curriculum? Well, not too long ago, a real horror story was making the rounds: teachers, if you had your choice, would you choose a computer or a complete volume of Shakespeare works? "The teachers answered THE COMPUTER! (Just like the elementary school principal who traded her stage for a computer room...)

Let's hope it's a short-lived horror story. And I really do not think many reputable liberal arts colleges will join the few who now do not require their English majors to have courses in Shakespeare. Not all liberal-arts teachers will agree with me, however. Francis Conroy, a professor of Burlington County College in Pemberton NJ writes: "There is widespread agreement that public education since the 1970's has not been good enough. But do we really think we are going to improve learning with the current trend of more computers, tests and accountability alone? What we liberal- arts teachers have been through the past two decades has drained us of our richness. Almost all our resources have been siphoned off into technology and mechanization. If there is no richness left, how will making us more accountable help?"

I had clipped this article by Professor Conroy a few months ago–just before I was going out to LA. From Newport

Beach CA there had been reprinted a letter-to-the editor that Gerry Long had written. She started off, saying Leon Botstein's ideas have great validity but they should be taken even further than the American high school. Actually, all of society has been corrupted by the same things that corrupt high school education—the mass movement away from the study of anything that can't be quantified statistically.

"Our heroes are judged by the numbers—for selling the most albums, earning the most money in sports, gaining the most yards. Worst of all the prevailing attitude among adults is "If I own stock in General Electric, then I don't give a darn how much trash they give us on NBC, as long as they keep up the stock value."

"It stems from the obsession with sports and money, and is the result of moving away from teaching art, literature and philosophy at all levels."

As I was reading, I felt that every liberal arts college should receive a copy of this letter. And I suddenly remembered a recent conversation I had had back East. I was talking with a math teacher from a neighboring High School which in the days when I had plays competing would often be our stiff competition.

I asked the math teacher," Who is directing your plays nowadays? I know Mr. Stoner has retired. The gentleman gave a funny little chuckle.

"You know, I've been there six years already. I really don't know."

He was not embarrassed that he didn't know. Perhaps he loved his math (as I felt he should), but not to communicate with other faculty, nor to ever see some of his students in a fine play or musical????!!!!!

No doubt some problems of school reform rest with communication.

"Let us not look back in anger or forward in fear, but around in awareness."
                    -James Thurber